TRIBAL DEVELOPMENT: ISSUES AND POLICY OPTIONS

TRIBAL DEVELOPMENT
ISSUES AND POLICY OPTIONS

Prof. S.N. Tripathy

ANMOL PUBLICATIONS PVT. LTD.
NEW DELHI - 110 002 (INDIA)

ANMOL PUBLICATIONS PVT. LTD.
H.O.: 4374/4B, Ansari Road, Darya Ganj,
New Delhi-110 002 (India)
Ph.: 23278000, 23261597
B.O.: No. 1015, Ist Main Road, BSK IIIrd Stage
IIIrd Phase, IIIrd Block,
Bangalore - 560 085 (India)
Visit us at: www.anmolpublications.com

Tribal Development: Issues and Policy Options

First Published, 2007

ISBN 978-81-261-3478-6

PRINTED IN INDIA

Printed at Mehra Offset Press, Delhi.

Contents

Preface

Papers included in this volume are based on my past research works in the field of social science on multi-dimensional aspects of tribal development in the state of Orissa. Some of the papers were written in response to invitation for presentation in the national or state level seminars during the last two year. Also some published works on tribal issues were selected to incorporate in a single volume in this work.

While putting these researches write ups in a comprehensive volume attempts have been made to update them keeping the theme of the papers unaltered. Even though some outdated features could not be eliminated but it is anticipated that the researchers in the field will certainly find it immensely useful for further works in the field as it provides the base for such endeavours.

Thus, the study has been analyzed from macro to micro and will be immensely helpful to anthropologists, planners, policy-makers, researchers, tribal administrators and general readers.

I take this opportunity to express my gratitude to Professor Prahallad Panda, and Professor Gyana Chandra Kar my research and D.Litt. guide respectively.

I would like to record my sincere appreciation to my wife Meera, my son Sameer and daughter Sumita who have always provided me love and affection and congenial work environment during the preparation of this work.

I will also remain grateful to various organizations, persons for making me resourceful in materials for the present work. In this regard I express my gratitude to the Librarian, National Library, Kolkata, Librarian Orissa State Library, Bhubaneswar, NKC

Centre for Development Studies, Bhubaneswar, Librarian, Bureau of Statistics and Economics, Bhubaneswar (Orissa).

I am personally grateful to my friends and well wishers like Dr. Rati Kanta Acharjya, Dr. Chitrasen Pasayat, Dr. K.S. Bhat, regional Director, CSD, Hyderabad and others who are my constant source of inspiration.

I will be failing my duty if I do not express my heart-felt thanks to the respondent migrant households whose information have enriched this work.

Last but not the least, I am thankful to Mr. Kripal D. Joshi of Anmol Publications Pvt. Ltd., New Delhi whose persistent and personal effort has made this project to come to light.

—*Dr. S.N. Tripathy*

1

The Role of Sericulture for the Development of KBK Tribals (Orissa)*

The tribal population constitutes about 8.8 percent of the population of the country. Next to undivided Madhya Pradesh, Orissa has the highest concentration of tribal population in India. There are 62 tribes in Orissa constituting about 23 percent of the total population of the state.

The tribals in Orissa continued to remain socially, economically and educationally backward and are languishing at the bottom of the socio-economic ladder. Their geographical isolation and improvised economy have made them object of exploitation by the non-tribals. The powerful external forces of moneylenders, contractors and officials having their link with political personnel and police could exert dominant control over the tribals. The poverty-stricken, illiterate, innocent tribals fail to withstand the forces and become the prey to all types of exploitation.

Over- dependence on subsistence and uncertain agriculture, absence of rural non-farm employment, increasing deforestation, and recurring droughts have resulted in abject poverty of in the tribal dominated districts of Kalahandi, Bolangir and Koraput

*Paper presented in the KVI Commission sponsored national seminar, February,19, 2006 Department of Business Administration, Utkal University, Bhubaneswar, Orissa.

(KBK). Especially there are repeated cases sale of child, bonded labour, starvation death, frequent outbreak of diseases, mass drop-outs, migration, etc. in KBK districts (Tripathy, 1989).

It is well known that Orissa is one of the poverty-stricken states of India, where the magnitude of rural poverty has been the highest all along. The poverty ratios of different states for rural and urban areas in the years 1973-74, 1977-78, 1983, 1987-88 and 1993-94, 1999-2000 reveal that Orissa was always at higher stage of poverty ratios compared to the national average as well as most of the other states in India (Orissa Development Report: 267). It is also remarkable to note that the incidence of poverty is the highest among the tribal population in Orissa, which is as high as 80 percent in some parts of the state.

Despite concerted planned efforts India remained predominantly agricultural with 70 percent of its population remaining in rural villages under condition of inequality in the distribution of income and wealth, underemployment and poverty. Rapid growth of population resulted in pressure on scarce land resources leading to subdivision of land holdings, low productivity, meagre income, underemployment and finally, culminating migration of rural population to urban areas.

Khadi and village industries provide the key to minimize these problems by raising employment, income and ameliorate the conditions of poor. KVI has the advantage of meeting the demands of mass consumption goods with simple tools, low capital investments and use of local raw materials (Tripathy, 2000 132-135).

Despite planned efforts there has been wide disparity in the distribution of income and wealth, gains of development disproportionately percolating to the tribal concentrated backward regions of the country.

Intensive Development of Sericulture in KBK Districts

Sericulture presents a picture of well-knit agro-based cottage industry one of the most labour intensive employment oriented rural industries in our country. Sericulture is mainly two types: mulberry and non-mulberry. Non-mulberry sericulture includes tasar, eri, and muga. All the above category of Sericulture has been practiced in the tribal districts of Orissa. The district-wise position of sericulture cultivation in Orissa has been presented in the Table 1.1.

Table 1.1

District-wise position of sericulture cultivation in Orissa

Tasar	Mulberry	ERi
Mayurbhanj, Keonjhar, Sundergarh, Deogarh, Dhankanal	Gajapati, Koraput, Phulbani, Keonjhar, Nayagarh, Mayurbhanj, Rayagada	Cuttack, Sundargarh, Keonjhar, Phulbani, Sambalpur, Kalahandi, Koraput, Jagatsingpur

Source: Govt. of India, central silk board, upgradation of status paper on sericulture in Orissa for 1999-2000, Bhubaneswar

Thus, sericulture programme has been taken up widely in the rural areas of KBK districts as it provides ample scope for better earning of the rural people. It is proposed to take up mulberry sericulture in Koraput, Rayagada & Kalahandi districts for the development of the rural people. The tasar programme has also been taken up in Nuapada district to provide employment to the tribal people by way of tasar silk-worm rearing and production of tasar cocoons. The eri plantation and eri-silk worm rearing has also been taken up in Rayagada and Kalahandi districts. The objective is to provide self-employment to the interested farmers of these areas under the ongoing schemes of tassar, Mulberry and Eri.

Production of tasar cocoon and marketing of silk products has been a major livelihood option of the tribal farmers of the Sundargarh, Keonjhar, Mayurbhanj, Dhenkanal, Angul, Sambalpur, Deogarh, Boudh, Nuapada, Jajpur districts and weavers of Sambalpur, Sonepur, Cuttack, Jajpur, Keonjhar, Ganjam, Kalahandi, Bolangir and Koraput districts of Orissa.

In the year 1962, the responsibility of silk cocoon production, marketing and its promotion in Orissa was vested on an Apex Cooperative Society known as Orissa State Tasar & Silk Cooperative Society Ltd., (OST&SCS) which has been renamed as Orissa

Cooperative Tasar & Silk Federation Ltd., (SERIFED), where 62 primary TRCS, 36 MRCS and 60 Silk WCS were the members. It has provided employment opportunity to 35,462 ST, 30,957 SC and 4,505 OBC families in silk worm rearing and 30,000 families in silk reeling and weaving. It provided both forward and backward linkages to silk producing rearers and weavers.

Sericulture provides self-employment opportunity to the tribal/BPL families through plantation of trees like Assan & Arjun for utilization in silkworm rearing and production of tassar cocoons. Besides, up-gradation of degraded forest land for tassar culture there is a potentiality of generating periodical income to the farmers all-round the year through mulberry silkworm activity and getting leaf from mulberry garden.

Sericulture, which comes under the scope of KVI sector, generates direct and indirect employment in various ways. Cocoon production uses mulberry leaf as an input and hence provides employment in the forms of mulberry growers.

Operations Performed by Tribals

The nature of operations performed by women are:

1. Picking of leaves from the garden and carrying the leaves to the places of silk worm rearing.
2. Chopping of the leaves into small pieces, square in shape, to make it convenient for the worms to eat them at the corners and above to reduce the wastage in leaves.
3. Feeding leaves to worms.
4. Cleaning wooden trays and round bamboo trays.
5. Application of manure to mulberry plants, removal of weeds etc. in the field.
6. Sweeping the rooms where silkworms are kept, fetching water and sprinkling it to make the room cool, applying medicine to protect the worm from the ants etc.
7. Mounting and harvesting of cocoons. Thus 60% of the labour requirements of the sericulture are provided by tribals particularly women.

The objectives of the SERIFED Society are to organize and develop the sericulture industry in Orissa on a Cooperative basis and to expand market for sericulture products i.e. Cocoons, Yarn and Fabrics in and outside the State. To attain these objectives, the SERIFED Ltd. should have a sound economic foundation so as to arrange fund for carrying on business, to provide financial and other assistance to the member societies for raising silk worm food plantations, rearing of silk worm, reeling and spinning of cocoons and weaving of silk fabrics.

Secondly, to take lease from the forest department for rearing of tasar silkworm and collection of tasar cocoons for the society on behalf of the members.

Thirdly, the objective of the society is to fix gradation and purchase price of tasar and mulberry cocoons, to arrange for procurement, lifting and marketing of cocoons, reeled yarn and fabrics inside and outside the state without prejudice to the interests of the member society.

Fourthly, the society aims at arranging training of the villagers, members of the primary societies, personnel of the society and Govt. department in various aspects of sericulture.

At present there are 39,280 farmers in 62 numbers of Primary tasar rearing cooperative societies (TRCS), 7,320 farmers in 36 mulberry rearing cooperative societies(MRCS) and 8,230 weavers through 61 weavers cooperative societies (WCS) getting proper marketing facilities to sale their products through SERIFED.

It is therefore imperative to overcome the bottlenecks and also develop the skill, knowledge, and awareness among tribals coupled with income generating labour intensive KVI in tribal concentrated KBK districts of Orissa, through the development of sericulture — which can bring about a catalytic change in their socio-economic condition (Tripathy, 2004, p.105)

NOTES AND REFERENCES

1. KBK districts basically refer to the undivided districts such as Kalahandi, Bolangir and Koraput and newly organized eight districts of Orissa namely:

(i) Kalahandi. (ii) Nuapara (iii) Bolangir (iv) Sonepur (v) Koraput (vi) Nawarangpur (vii) Malkanagiri and (viii) Rayagada, which are among the most backward districts of India.

Total Area in sq.km: 47646

Total population: 63,20,4.68 (19.96% to total state population)

S.T. population: 24, 48,301(38.73% to total KBK population)

S.C. population: 10, 00,840(15.83% to total KBK population)

2. Tripathy, S.N. (1989), Bonded labour in India, Discovery Publishing House, New Delhi

3. Tripathy, S.N. (2000), KVI for Rural Development, in Self-edited *Rural Development*, Discovery Publishing House, New Delhi

4. Tripathy, S.N. (2004), Development of tribal women through non-farm employment in Orissa, in self-edited *Tribal Women in India*, Dominant Publishers and Distributors, New Delhi.

5. Orissa Development Report (2002), Planning Commission, Government of India, New Delhi.

2

RRBs and Agriculture in WTO Regime*

Despite vast expansion of the formal credit system in India, the dependence of rural poor on moneylenders continues in some areas particularly in tribal regions of the state. For various reasons the credit flow to these sections of the population for meeting their credit requirements could not be institutionalized. This was due to the factors like inadequate supply of credit, demand-supply gap, improper identification of beneficiaries and unhealthy competition from informal credit agencies (Tripathy, 2004, 2006).

Many studies in the past have established that institutional credit has bypassed small farmers, the landless and the non-cultivators. These landless people in rural sector need credit mainly to meet the deficiencies in income for basic consumption and over come occasional emergencies. The formal institutional lending does not match the requirements to maximum rural people, as a result of which they are to depend on traders and money - lenders (Subas C Kumar, 2001, pp. 106-107).

The important objective of a Regional Rural Bank as has been postulated by Narashimha Committee was to provide credit facilities to the small and marginal farmers, rural artisans and other weaker sections of the rural sector. Prior to the establishment of these banks the institutional agencies contributed only 20 % of the credit needs of the rural sector and the rest supplied by the

*Paper presented in the UGC sponsored state level seminar in the Department of Commerce, UNS Mahavidyalaya, Mugpal, Jajpur, Orissa

private moneylenders. The rural banks have been established in every district to fill up this credit gap and to provide cheaper credit to the weaker sections of the society.

In the district of Ganjam, the regional rural bank was established known as Rushikulya Gramya Bank (RGB) on 14th February 1981. The district is a high-density region of the state with about 70 % of people depending on agriculture and more than 60 % farmers belonging to the category of small and marginal farmers.

Indian agriculture would be facing a serious challenge, both internal and external, in WTO-regime. It is characterized by stagnating yield at a low level, a very large proportion of marginal, smail and semi-medium holdings, burdened with high proportion of labour force and highly concentrated cropping pattern. Over the period of time, the share of agriculture in GDP has decreased.

However, the desired shift of labour force, from agriculture to other sectors could not take place. All this, together with pressure of population, has resulted in low exportable surplus. These limitations along with liberalized trade scenario backed by WTO-regime, would adversely affect the global competitiveness of Indian agriculture.

In order to meet the challenges of the world trade and search out better opportunities for our agricultural exports, we need a huge investment in agriculture to boost up the productivity and output with special preference to export-oriented agricultural crops. In the context of WTO regime, there is an imperative need for setting up the export oriented farms for selected agricultural commodities particularly for plantation crops and spices and providing them incentives particularly to the small and marginal products, special encouragements like duty free import of capital goods and other requirements to 100 percent export oriented units, promotion of value-added products (A.Sailaja, 2006). These could be possible through a massive investment in agricultural sector.

Government's participation in agricultural marketing should also be increased to the required extent. Intensive efforts should be made to conduct the survey and analytical studies of world-wide agricultural marketing. Further, the Government should have a comprehensive product-wise policy with long run consistency. The Central and State Governments should work in co-ordination to increase agricultural production and exportable surplus through agricultural investment in providing liberal and timely credit to the farmers. All institutional sources of credit starting from the apex level of NABARD to Regional Rural Banks should allocate adequate funds for agricultural sector to cater to the needs of the agriculturists.

There exists a large potential for increasing export of quite a few agricultural commodities produced in India. However, despite the great potentials for increase in agricultural exports, various economists suggest caution in completely freeing exports, especially of food grains to other countries. There is a need to regulate the exports, not only for reason of food security but also for some other politico-economic considerations. Specific steps have to be earnestly taken to generate this surplus. This implies development of infrastructure especially provision of agricultural credit, irrigation and power research, extension of new technology to uncovered crops and areas, development of market infrastructure and a more efficient use of existing resources (A.Sailaja, 2006).

Import of agricultural commodities unrelated to the security of these commodities in the country will only mean a wasteful use of foreign exchange. Another reason for overseeing the imports of agricultural commodities is the need to ensure that the imported agricultural commodities are not hoarded for profiteering by the private individuals. Besides development of infrastructure, multinationals can be allowed to develop agro-processing industries. But we have to be very cautious while recommending such a step for some other productive activities allied to agriculture.

There is need to change the rural mindset on agro-exports. A farmer as well as a laborers working in the field should be made to think about export and quality of the product. The industry should provide agro-business services to the farming community. A rural infrastructure development fund, adequate flow of credit to agriculture is some of the steps in this direction can support the landless labourers, small and marginal farmers.

Thus, there is an urgent need to evolve appropriate policy measures and undertake a serious research so that ways and means could be found out to prepare the Indian agriculture for the fast changing domestic and global scenario under the WTO regime. We would have to devise a multi-pronged policy and strategy to face the challenge and make Indian agriculture sustainable and competitive (A.Sailaja, 2006)

Table 2.1

Sector- wise Loans Issued by RGB during 2002 to 2005 (Rs. in lakhs)

Sector-wise Loans	As on 31.3.2002	As on 31.3.2003	As on 31.3.2004	As on 31.3.2005
Crop loan	1436.12 (24.82)	2399.43	2489.21	3547.36 (38.07)
ATL and allied activities	128.94 (2.22)	220.54	366.41	669.71 (7.18)
SSI	132.10 (2.28)	171.18	185.29	193.29 (2.07)
Service sector	1408.63 (24.35)	1553.25	2046.42	2287.48 (24.55)
Others	2678.22 (46.70)	2743.60	3481.53	2619.17 (28.11)
Total	5784.00 (100.00)	7088.00 (100.00)	8568.86 (100.00)	9317.01 (100.00)

Note: Figures in parentheses are percentage to total.

Source: Annual Reports of Rushikulya Gramya Bank, Head Office, Berhampur, Ganjam (Orissa) No.21, 22, 23, 24

It is revealed from the table that there has been increase in the amount of investment of fund in all categories of loans except in the category "others".

The agricultural sector has been accorded more priority has been displayed from the Table 2.1.

Table 2.2

Recovery position of RGB (Amount in lakhs) As on June 2002

Sector	Demand	Collection	Balance	% of Overdues
ST Agricultural loan	1736.49	1278.16	485.33	26.39
Agricultural term loan	299.32	160.92	138.40	46.24
Allied activities	201.30	72.62	128.68	63.92
Non-agricultural loans	2240.34	1400.07	840.27	37.51
Total	4477.45	2911.77	1566.65	34.97

Recovery position of RGB (Amount in lakhs) As on June 2003

Sector	Demand	Collection	Balance	% of Overdues
ST Agricultural loan	2336.32	1585.27	751.05	32.15
Agricultural term loan	328.42	205.97	122.45	37.19
Allied activities	326.63	116.17	120.46	50.91
Non-agricultural loans	2509.87	1638.81	871.36	34.72
Total	5411.24	3554.92	1865.32	34.48

Recovery position of RGB (Amount in lakhs) As on June 2004

Sector	Demand	Collection	Balance	% of Overdues
ST Agricultural loan	3104.30	2292.84	811.46	26.14
Agricultural term loan	485.15	278.25	179.90	39.27
Allied activities	231.15	68.71	162.44	70.27
Non-agricultural loans	3040.34	1957.35	1082.99	35.62
Total	6833.94	4597.15	2236.79	32.73

Source: As indicated in the table 2.1.

The position of bank recovery has been exhibited in the Table 2.2.

The position of recovery indicates that there has been a remarkable progress in the recovery of bank loans during the period.

Recovery of Loans

Timely recovery of loan is a major problem of RGB in the

country. The RGB being a rural development bank and has been rendering its services as per government guidelines for investment of its funds. Therefore, its administrative expenditures are to be curtailed so as to make them viable and cost effective. From the point of provision of agricultural credit it has played a commendable role and thus, helping the development of the rural economy.

Besides from the regular recovery, the RGB has accorded additional thrust to improve the recovery position more particularly in non-performing assets (NPAs) through various policy decisions and recovery measures especially by organizing of mass recovery camps, lok adalats, seizure of assets, auction of pledged gold ornaments and compromise settlements. The reduction of NPA assumed vital importance in improving the profitability of the bank.

REFERENCES

1. A. Sailaja Devi (2006), "WTO and Indian Agriculture", in Tripathy, S.N. (ED.) *Rural Development for Social Change*, Discovery Publishing House, New Delhi
2. Subas c Kumar (2001), Dispensing credit for rural development in India, *The Fourth World-Journal of Marginalized People*, NISWASS, Bhubaneswar, No.14, October.
3. Tripathy, S. N. (2004), "Evaluating women self- help groups in tribal Orissa' in self edited *'Tribal Women in India'*, Dominant Publishers and Distributors, New Delhi.
4. Tripathy, S. N. (2006), "Rural finance and self- Help Groups", in R. K. Sahoo and Tripathy, S.N. (ed.) *Self- Help Group and Women Empowerment*, Anmol Publications Pvt. Ltd., New Delhi.

3

Rural Credit and RRBs in India*

At the dawn of Independence, cooperatives were the only formal financial institutions providing credit in rural areas. In view of the poor outreach and other inefficiencies, the All India Rural Credit Survey Report (1954) had observed, "cooperation has failed but cooperation must succeed". During the fifties and early sixties, despite a massive expansion of both short-term and long-term co-operative banks in the country, the share of formal credit in the rural sector was far from satisfactory.

The All India Rural Debt and Investment Survey Report 1971 revealed that in 1961, the share of institutional credit in rural households was only 17.3 per cent. The reluctance of formal financial institutions to venture into the rural hinterland and finance agriculture, small industries and business enterprises considered as risky and unprofitable.

Although agriculture continues to occupy an important position in the Indian economy, its share in GDP has declined from 44.8% in 1977-78 to only 27.6% in 1999-2000 at constant 1993-94 prices. However, there has been very little decline in agriculture's share in employment. The share of employment in agriculture (UPSS) declined from 73.9% in 1972-73 to 60.2% by 1999-2000 (Table 3.1).

*Paper presented in the UGC sponsored state level seminar in the Department of Commerce, UNS Mahavidyalaya, Mugpal, Jajpur, Orissa

Table 3.1

Share of Agriculture in GDP and Employment

Year	% Share of agriculture in GDP at 1993-94 prices	% Share of agriculture in employment (UPSS)
1972-73	44.8	73.9
1993-94	33.5	63.9
1999-2000	27.6	60.2

Sources: National Accounts Statistics and survey on employment and unemployment-various rounds.

Thus, agriculture being the backbone of Indian economy the Government had to make certain policy pronouncements for catering to the credit needs of the rural India.

It was with the advent of nationalization of banks in 1969 that commercial financial institutions were considered as the potential instruments to be applied for agricultural and all round development of rural India. The premise was that credit for the rural people would provide an impetus to the process of agricultural and finally, rural development. During the next fifteen years, the strategy adopted for expanding credit flow to the rural economy revolved around the following broad strategies.

Firstly, there was a conscious attempt for expansion of commercial banks, particularly in rural areas. The branch licensing policy of Reserve Bank of India (RBI) was aggressively used for this purpose. While the total number of bank branches in the country has exhibited an increase from 8,832 to 53,165 between June 1969 and June 1985, the share of rural branches in the total bank branches increased from 22.2 per cent to 58.74 per cent during the same period. The population served per bank branch office declined from 64,000 to 15,000.

Secondly, an era of directed credit through the concept of priority sector was ushered in, under which prescriptions were laid down for banks to lend a certain percentage of their credit to sectors such as agriculture, small-scale industries and to the weaker sections of the society. As a result of which, domestic banks were advised to ensure that not less than one-third of their outstanding credit should be directed to the priority sector by March 1979. Consequently, the advances of public sector banks to the priority sector, which formed 14.6 per cent of their total advances in June 1969, rose to form 34.0 per cent of their total advances in December 1979.

In 1980, banks were advised to ensure 40 per cent of their net bank credit (NBC) went to the priority sector by March 1985. Within the priority sector, a separate sub-target was fixed for agriculture and allied activities. Banks were advised to achieve the sub-target for agriculture at 15 per cent of their NBC by March 1985, which was gradually enhanced to 18 per cent by March 1990. The emphasis on agriculture and priority sector credit led to the introduction of penalties for non-achievement of priority sector targets by banks.

In 1994, the Government set up the Rural Infrastructure Development Fund (RIDF) under which, domestic banks fell short of achieving the priority sector targets were required to deposit amounts specified by RBI on a year-to-year basis. Similarly, foreign banks with priority sector shortfall were required to deposit the amount of shortfall with the Small Industries Development Bank of India (SIDBI). As a result of all these measures, the priority sector advances of all scheduled commercial banks increased significantly towards the late eighties.

Regional Rural Banks and Rural Credit

The most remarkable development in the sphere of agricultural credit was the birth of a new category of banks - Regional Rural Banks (RRBs), created to develop the rural economy by providing credit and other facilities to agriculture, trade, industry and other productive activities in the rural areas. Launched in 1975, RRBs were expected to combine local feel and familiarity with the rural problems, which the cooperatives possessed on the one hand, and degree of business, organization and modern outlook of commercial banks on the other. Thus, regional rural banks was designed to help cooperatives in order to strengthen the existing multi- agency rural credit system and building a strong resource base and increase the out reach of commercial banks in rural areas.

These banks multiplied rapidly and had 12,602 branches ten years later. In 1989, there were 196 RRBs with 14,651 branches. While the number of RRBs has remained unchanged since then, the number of branches has changed only marginally. As on 31st March 1999, there were 196 RRBs functioning in 476 districts in the country with a network of 14498 branches. Thus, with the introduction of RRBs, banking facilities were brought much closer to the rural population to cater to the requirements of rural agricultural sector of India.

All these measures resulted in a massive flow of institutional credit to the rural sector. According to the All India Debt and Investment Survey, 1991-92, the share of institutional credit in the indebtedness of rural households rose significantly from 29.2 per cent in 1971 to 61.2 percent in 1981. Within this, the share of commercial banks increased from 2.2 per cent in 1971 to 28.0 percent in 1981.

The setting up of the National Bank for Agriculture and Rural Development (NABARD) in 1982 as an apex financial institution for promoting, monitoring and refinancing the rural financial system was another significant milestone in the journey of strengthening credit flow to the rural economy of India.

The purpose wise advances made by RRBs during a period of 1982 to 1998 have been depicted in the Table 3.2. It is evident that in 1982, out of the total advances 60.10 % of loans were advanced to farm sector and 26.92 % of loans were forwarded to rural artisans and retail trade.

In 1998, the percentages of loans to farm sector had declined and it was 47.49 % of the total advances. On the other hand the advances to non- farm sector had recorded 31.68 % (an increase of 4.76 % over the year 1982).

An Evaluation of Rural Credit

While the strategies followed undoubtedly helped to build up a broad-based institutional infrastructure for delivery and deployment of credit, the emphasis throughout was on achieving certain quantitative targets. As a consequence, inadequate attention was paid to the qualitative aspects involved and certain weaknesses began to manifest themselves in the fabric of rural credit.

Tabl 3.2

Year-wise and purpose wise classification of direct advances of Regional rural banks

Years	Short-term crop loans	Agricultural investments	Rural artisans/ village cottage industries	Retail Trade/ business self-employment	Consumption lons	Other purpose	Indirect advances	Total
1982	108.64 (18.83)	238.20 (41.27)	30.63 (5.31)	124.70 (21.61)	2.62 (0.45)	46.91 (8.13)	25.41 (4.40)	577.11 (100.00)
1985	264.16 (18.77)	551.40 (39.17)	79.90 (5.68)	366.00 (26.00)	10.90 (0.77)	101.85 (7.24)	33.46 (2.37)	1407.67 (100.00)
1990	615.52 (17.32)	1222.51 (34.40)	276.47 (7.78)	1051.72 (29.59)	54.15 (1.52)	289.97 (8.16)	43.71 (1.23)	3554.04 (100.00)
1991	644.95 (16.96)	1205.19 (31.69)	320.75 (8.43)	1143.61 (30.07)	43.15 (1.13)	411.19 (10.81)	34.76 (0.91)	3609.27 (100.00)
1992	678.78 (16.59)	1305.48 (31.91)	349.01 (8.53)	1219.15 (29.80)	40.13 (0.98)	459.56 (11.24)	38.74 (0.95)	4090.86 (100.00)
1993	802.07 (17.34)	1472.49 (31.83)	380.01 (8.21)	1298.84 (28.07)	89.42 (1.93)	552.19 (11.63)	31.71 (0.69)	4626.73 (100.00)
1994	886.67 (16.88)	1673.10 (31.85)	443.79 (8.45)	1368.82 (26.06)	108.03 (2.06)	739.27 (14.07)	33.33 (0.63)	5253.02 (100.00)
1995	1115.09 (17.73)	1893.84 (30.10)	523.29 (8.32)	1555.21 (24.72)	181.87 (2.89)	988.87 (15.72)	32.80 (0.52)	6290.96 (100.00)
1996	1308.25 (17.43)	2185.26 (28.76)	586.40 (7.81)	1836.39 (24.47)	257.81 (3.44)	1323.37 (17.63)	34.54 (0.46)	7505.02 (100.00)
1997	1631.70 (18.72)	2412.57 (27.67)	672.18 (7.71)	1972.30 (22.62)	381.07 (4.37)	1599.11 (18.34)	49.16 (0.57)	8718.08 (100.00)
1998	1913.92 (19.41)	2769.09 (28.08)	1229.61 (12.47)	1894.70 (19.21)	97.32 (0.99)	1943.69 (19.71)	12.49 (0.13)	9860.82 (100.00)

Note: Figures in parentheses are percentage to total.

Source: NABARD, Statistical Reports, RRB division.

The unbridled branch expansion began to affect the profitability of banks as most of the rural branches resulting in accumulated sizable losses. Directed credit prescriptions reduced the maneuverability of banks in their deployment of credit at a time when the reserve requirements of banks were also quite high. This, coupled with prescriptions of lower interest rates for priority sector loans, also contributed adversely to the bottom line of banks.

As the Report of the Committee on Financial System (Narasimham Committee) observed in 1991, the end result was the disturbing growth in over dues, which not only hampered the recycling of scarce resources of banks, but also affected the profitability and viability of the financial institutions (Table 3).

The RRBs, with a predominantly rural network, were the worst affected in this scenario and accumulated huge losses. During 1994-95, only 32 of the 196 RRBs made profit while the accumulated losses of RRBs aggregated Rs 1,686.61 crore as at the end of March 1995 (Bhatia and Bhatia, 2005).

The Government sponsored schemes witnessed extremely poor recovery rates. Misutilisation of subsidy was exceedingly high and repayment ethics were thrown to the winds. The repayment rate under the IRDP remained less than 33 per cent and the programme created about 40 million bank defaulters (Fisher and Sriram: 2002).

And the Government's disastrous Agricultural Debt Relief Scheme of 1989 put the final nail in the coffin; and has been considered as one of the major impediments to poor recovery and credit discipline.

Financial sector reforms and rural credit

With the advent of financial sector reforms commencing from the early nineties, the weaknesses of the earlier measures began to manifest themselves. The health of the banking system had deteriorated with banks being saddled with a huge weight of non-performing assets (NPAs), unviable branches and enormous losses (Bhatia and Bhatia, 2005). Stories of leakages from the subsidy-linked credit programmes were legendary and it was widely

Table 3.3

Number of Profit and loss making RRBs during 1994-95 to1998-99 (Rs. in Crore)

Year	Total no. of RRBs	RRBs Making profit	Amount of profit	Profit per unit	RRBs making loss	Amount of loss	Loss per unit	Accumulated loss
1994-95	196	32 (11.73)	21.91	0.95	173	388.87	2.25	1691.72
1995-96	196	45 (22.96)	42.44	0.94	151	465.37	3.08	2176.08
1996-97	196	44 (22.45)	69.68	1.58	152	881.07	5.80	3052.67
1997-98	196	126 (64.29)	304.22	2.41	70	230.57	3.29	3116.20
1998-99	196	147 (75.00)	425.90	2.89	49	178.10	3.69	3100.10

Note: Figures in parenthesis are percentage to total.
Source: NABARD, 1999.

conceived that only a small fraction of the credit actually percolated to the deserving.

It is evident from the table 3.3 that though the number of loss making RRBS has declined from 152 to 49, the loss per unit has increased from 2.25 to 3.69 crore during the period 1994-95 to 1998-99.

As of late 1990s about 32 percent of the rural households, particularly economically weaker sections are indebted to the moneylenders and their lending was rarely for any productive investments. For any kind of economic activity some sort of financial service is indispensable no matter how rudimentary it was.

In their effort to eradicate poverty and develop the rural economy a wide network of rural bank branches have been involved in implementing a wide variety of poverty alleviation programmes.

However, a very large number of poor remained outside the fold of the formal banking system and perhaps it could be due to the fact that the deposit and loan products are not ideally suited to meet the most immediate requirements of the poor (RBI, 2004).

REFERENCES

1. Bhatia, Navin and Bhatia, Anju, Financial Institutions as Change Agents for Rural Development - The New Paradigm, Paper presented in the NIRD FOUNDATION-DAY SEMINAR, RURAL DEVELOPMENT AND SOCIAL CHANGE, Hyderabad, 9-10 November 2005
2. Fisher, Thomas and M.S.Sriram (2002), Beyond Micro-Credit: Putting Development Back into Micro-Finance, Vistaar Publications, New Delhi.
3. Reserve Bank of India (2004): Report of the Advisory Committee on Flow of Credit to Agriculture and Related Activities from the Banking System, Mumbai, June

4

The Socio-Cultural Features of Saoras of Gajapati*

The tribals who constitute about 8 percent of country's total population are concentrated in more than 21 states and five union territories. The tribals are the most vulnerable among the weaker sections of the community. Because of their abject poverty, ignorance, simplicity and illiteracy, the middlemen, traders and contractors exploit the tribals.

The moneylenders have been charging exorbitant rates of interest from them. Traders have been buying their produce at rock bottom prices and selling it at very high rates, thus, exploiting them in both ways. The contractors have been paying them very low wages.

Two things are of greatest importance to tribals, i.e. land and forest. The tribal people are either hunters or forest food gatherers, settled or hill cultivators, shepherds or craftsmen. They cultivate the lands by means of traditional methods and thus get very low returns. As a result, these people live in a bare subsistence economy. But there is something inherent in the tribal philosophy, which has kept these people, content with fulfillment of their necessities. Economic exploitation of tribals have resulted in heavy migrations, value adulterations, increased bonded labourers and subversive activities.

***This paper constitutes a part of the research work undertaken by the author during 2003-04. A detailed account of Lanjia Soura, socio-economic and demographic profile, has been published in a book form, "Primitive Tribes of India", Anmol Publications Pvt. Ltd., New Delhi, 2006.**

The tribals are exploited in various ways. The most important form of tribal exploitation is alienating them from their lands by non-tribals. Thus, in the recent past the landless tribals are growing in numbers.

The landless tribal labourers are the cheap source of labour supply for non-tribal agriculturalists and plantation works. The tribal labourer is paid less then the non-tribals and they are also not given other benefits as permissible under labour legislation by their employers.

The tribals exchange their little forest produce for other goods and services with the help of businessmen of nearby villages and towns. So, it is very easy for the businessmen to exploit the tribals by offering a throw away price.

Review of Literature

The Commission on the Backward Classes (1955) stated that the present problem of backwardness is due to variety of causes-social, environmental, economic and political and have operated both openly and in a subtle form for centuries. Economic backwardness is the result and not the cause of many social evils of the present day.

Somalwar (1980) in his paper highlighted the condition of tribes of Maharastra state. He has expressed that the resources available in tribal areas optimally utilized to facilitate decent living standard of tribes. He has pointed out that in tribal regions there are instances, which indicate that loans distributed to tribes for agriculture and other purposes are much less than recorded in the official files. Tribes are not aware of the schemes launched by the government / the government is also not very keen to publicize it widely. Because of illiteracy, tradition and customs, the tribes look at the schemes in a prejudiced manner. Further, he has pointed out that government machinery and their men have failed to understand the tribal problems.

Dr. Singh (1984) makes a significant contribution to the study of Sauras a little known isolated tribe living in Ganjam (undivided) and Koraput — (undivided) districts of Orissa. The author traces the history of tribe from its isolated autonomous existence in the eighteenth century, its subjugation by the British imperial power and accession to the oppressive hegemony of the muthadars and intermediaries, through prolonged exploitation, to the present day when their entire value systems is in a melting-pot. The study investigates the effect of introduction of Panchayati Raj with skill and meticulous care and remarked that the village councils of Saoras have survived ravages of various onslaughts. It has been concluded that the leading personalities emerging from the Panchayats have still to find their feet and that the traditional leadership is losing influence.

Narayan (1988) highlights the multi-dimensional changes, which took place in tribal Bihar during 1976-86.The various problems faced by the tribes are discussed and constructive suggestions for bettering their quality of life are made.

Paul (1989) explains the various dimensions of tribal movements with especial reference to 'Udayachal movement' in Assam valley. The author has suggested radical transformation of socio-economic system for removing inequality, injustice and exploitation.

Joshi (1990) remarks that regions have their own special problems and tribal regions in particular require a special approach. Extensive interviews and group discussions carried out in Jhabua district of Madhya Pradesh highlight the scanty as well as the over- used resources for development.

Jain (1991) focuses the social monuments among Bhils of Southern Rajasthan, who constitute the third largest group of tribals in the country providing a new insight to the tribal social movements, the study reveals a critique to the historical analysis of Bhils Social movements and their approach characterised by feudal attributes.

Chaudhuri (1992) unfolds the parameters of tribal economics understanding the attitudes/ responsiveness of various groups to the on- going socio-economic transition. The study explores tribal crafts, food gathering ventures, as well as recent land reforms, from technologies, agricultural income, forestry and the developmental role of the non-government intervention in district tribal situations.

Chaudhuri (1992) examines whether the sub-plan approach to tribal development is the best available strategy, also whether there is adequate concern in this thrust on induced change on crucial roles of forestry and ecology.

Chaudhuri (1992) critically analyses the literacy levels among different tribal groups. In-depth analysis of the curriculum for tribal youths, their reaction to the education being imparted, and the tribals' status in university education have been made in his study. The volume also examines the rationale behind the primitive groups' in responsive to formal education despite governmental incentives.

Patel (1993) observed that the demands of commerce and pressure on land have led inexorably to the influx of plain area people into the tribal areas, which subsequently has led to further exploitation of tribal people. Adding to their cup of owe, the year plans with their emphasis of public projects deepened the existing crisis by speeding up the displacement of tribals especially minor tribes, also known as primitive tribal groups despite a plethora of legislative measures, special safeguards and special developmental efforts, tribal rights in land and forests exploitation, reservation from peasantry class to labour, widespread displacement causing tribal tensions, loss of identity and lack of confidence have emerged as baffling problems for the tribes and policy makers.

Rao. M.K. (1993) in his research paper presents the changing scenario of tribals in Andhra Pradesh. He opines proper identification of ethnic boundaries of each tribal community is imperative in view of the extending of various developmental activities under various provisions of the constitution.

Mohanty (1994) focuses on the non- conventional approach to tribal development in various respects including education, culture, health care, forestry etc.and lists some special features for the UN declaration of the international year for the indigenous people of the world.

(Mrs). Ray (1997) in her paper focused socio-economic and cultural life of tribals in Orissa. She has pointed out that in Orissa, important tribes are Bhuiya, Kandh, Kolla, Gund, Ho, Santal, Savara, Jhanga, Parja, Munda, Kharria, Oraun etc.

The Bhuiyas are the wild tribes of the state of Orissa. They are found in Mayurbhanj, Keonjhar, Boud, and Kalahandi etc. The Bhuiyas claim to be use children of the soil (Bhui, earth) and to possess full property rights over the soil in the manner as other aboriginal tribes always term themselves Zamindars.

The Jhangs are the wild and primitive tribes found in Keonjhar, and Dhenkanal districts of Orissa.

The Kharrias are a tribe closely allied linguistically to the Jhangs. They are found in Simlipal and Meghasani hill ranges of Mayurbhanj district of Orissa.

The Saharas are found in Dhenkanal, Keonjhar, and Mayurbhanj districts of Orissa.

The life pattern of the tribes of Orissa depends upon the environment they live in and the resources available to them.

DR. Tripathy (1997) examined the problems and policies of Tribals in India. Uneconomic land holding, growth of middlemen, unorganised many market, defective borrowing system and the extravagant habit of tribals on ceremonial occasions have thrown the tribals into the hands of unscrupulous many lenders. The problem of illiteracy, ignorance and poverty aggravated the situation. Indebtedness among the tribals has economic and social dimensions. In many areas it leads to bonded ness due to debt descending from generation to generation.

Dr (Mrs.) Hemalatha Prasad (1997) examined the development of tribal women thrift society and grain Bank in Andhra Pradesh. The four Integrated Tribal development Agency (ITDA) covered in the study are Seethampete (Srikakulam district), Parvathipuram (Vizanagaram distriet), Paderu (Visakhapatnam district) and Ramapachodavaram (East Godavari district).

She has pointed out that women are burdened with a heavy workload because of their domestic duties, childcare in addition to the work of collecting fuel wood; fetch water and fodder for animals. The decline in the availability of founds, fuel and medicinal plants in the forests has an adverse effect on their health and nutritional status.

The tribal economy is subsistence, critically exposed to the vagaries of nature, and represents a hand to mouth and struggle for the tribal communities. Agrarian Savara are expert in terrace cultivation. They prepare platforms are over the other on the low gradient slopes and construct stone terraces in order to catch and preserve the down-flowing rain water usually from a hill stream.

The tribal economy in Andhra Pradesh is agro-forest based on subsistence agriculture the collection of forest produce. The tribals of Andhra Pradesh, known as Savara have been migrated from the neighbouring state of Orissa.

Participation of women in community activities particularly construction of cheek dams, School Buildings and Anganwadi centres helped them in gaining wage employment and also ensured them the quality of construction through elimination of private contractors.

High rate of matching grant in terms of cash towards their saying contribution motivated tribal women members to organise themselves into small thrift groups.

Dash (1997) evaluated the tribal development scenario of Orissa in the context of poverty amelioration programmes of the government. It has been felt that for integrating the various anti poverty programmes with the sectoral programmes in a specified area is needed so as to ensure a sustainable increase in employment and income of the rural poor and tribals.

It has been suggested that in the implementation of wage employment programmes priority should be given to activities which improve the land resources base and eco-system in rural areas such as water harvesting, desalting of irrigation tanks, construction of field canals, drainage and measures for soil conservation including afforestation.

Dr. N.C. Das and Dr.Sahu (1997) in their paper analyzed the changing socio- demographic scenario of the Savaras in Orissa. Saoras are mainly distributed in Ganjam, Gajapati and Koraput districts of Orissa. They are also found in the adjacent districts of Andhra Pradesh. There are three broad divisions of the tribe such as Lanjia (primitive), the Sudha (Hinduised) and the Christian (converted) Saoras. The latter two groups are the changed categories, where as the Lanjias are the primitive and the original Saoras.

The common identity of Lanjia Saora is expressed in their religious beliefs and rituals such as worship of common spirits and ghosts. This group mostly depends on shifting cultivation along with ford gathering as their livelihood. Economically, they are most backward compared to the other two groups.

The Sudha Saura exhibits many cultural features of the Hindus. They have accepted plane cultivation being influenced by the neighbouring Hindus. As a result the Sudha Saora villages are mostly found in the foothills. Besides, they also practice animal husbandry and various indigenous economic pursuits.

The Christian Sauras who have accepted Christianity belong to primitive (Lanjia) Section of the community. The adoption of a new religion has separated.

From the other two sections of the Saora, economically, the Christian Sauras are better of compared to their counterparts, as they receive donations, both in cash and kind, from the missionaries along with health and educational benefits. Further, despite their conversion to Christianity they also avail the government concessions and other facilities similar to primitive Sauras.

The study conducted by authors based on empirical work. The data have been collected from 218 Lanjia households, 212 sudha households and 227 Christian households from 26 villages through structured schedules. The schedules mainly contained variables like family size, distribution of population, educational Scenario, occupational status, income & expenditure, marital status and other demographic features. The study is confined to Mohana block of Chandragiri hills in Gajapati district of Orissa.

Masavi (1999) in his study focussed human resource development in tribal areas of Gujarat State. He stated that the role of education as an investment in human resources has been increasingly recognised all over the developing countries. It is revealed that although the spread of education in India as a whole has been quite fast in the last 5 decades, the spread of education among the scheduled tribes has been quite uneven.

Nagda (1999) studied the tribal health and development in Rajasthan State. He has pointed out that the tribal sub-plan approach was intended to narrow the gap between the levels of development of tribal and other areas. But despite the planned measures, literacy among women has been comparatively lower than male. The coverage of health facilities in tribal areas is comparatively less, especially in terms of population - doctor ratio and the number of hospital beds.

Tripathy (1999) examined the role of co-operatives for tribal development in Orissa. He has remarked that despite protective legislation's most of the tribals have remained in the grip of widespread poverty and exploitation. Inaccessibility of many tribal regions, inadequate facilities of assessing the impact of many development programmes on the tribal life and corruption at every stage of plan implementation has regulated in the backwardness and poverty of tribals. He has suggested that to bring the tribals under the co-operative fold it is imperative to relieve them from the clutches of the private many lenders -cum-traders so as to ameliorate the living standards of the tribals.

Bipin Kumar (2000) highlighted the problems of out migration among the tribals of Bihar. The cause leading to migration of tribals are rapid growth of population, worsening land-men ratio, lack of development, lack of non-agricultural work, poverty etc. The data were collected by undertaking survey and interview of the households from three districts Saurastipur, Patna and Bokaro. It was pointed out that most of the people who migrated were males. There is a new trend of exodus of rural youth not only from landless families but also from villages of Bihar.

It is needed to develop agriculture on modern lines and encourage non-farm employment opportunities in small and cottage industries so as to arrest the process of out-migration.

Pati (2000) analysed the communication strategy for tribal development. He has mentioned that the objective of any tribal development programmes must be for one provision of food, clothing, shelter, and education and health services for every one under conditions, which provide for universal dignity. Tribal development calls for a massive effort, not simply to boost production but to create and spread unemployment and to root out the fundamental causes of poverty, disease ignorance and injustice.

Development does not start with goods; it starts with people and their education, organisation and discipline. Without these elements, all resources remain latent and untapped potential.

Communication can't be seen in isolation but as a part of total development system. Both print and electronic media have got an important role to play for information dissemination and attitude formation. The question is that how people in distance remote areas will have adequate access to this important resource. The media should carry reputed message against passivity and withdrawal, against wrong health practices, against drug addiction, liquor and superstitions and against all types of social evils. Simultaneously the message should carry all development information highly credible for the mass.

Dash (2000) in his research write up focused the role of forests in the development of tribal Kendu leaf pluckers of Bolangir district (Orissa). He has started that the tribals of Orissa are economically and socially far backward then other social groups. Low rate of literacy, peculiar tradition and customs as well as their secluded existence is reinforced by hilly and forest surroundings keep them away from the main stay of our economy. In their tradition and customs forests play a significant role. From forest they gather materials afro housing, agricultural implements, trumpet, fuel, medicine, as well as collection of non-Tribal forest produces (NTFPs) like honey, lac, fruits, fodder, flowers, roots, gums, resin to provide them gainful employment & income.

As the Kendu leaf is the only surviving rotating forest produce which is providing employment and income are to people living in and around the forest areas helps to their upliftment in socio-economic condition and further processing of Kendu leaf to 'Bidi" may also provide more days of employment to the bidi rollers in the area, there should be conservation of forests. He further suggested that the Kendu leaf pluckers should be provided betters social security safety nets in order to alleviate their miserable living standard. Besides, there should be alternative avenues of employment and income.

Dr. Pasayat (2000) highlighting the need of educating tribal children in Orissa expressed that most of the tribal people reside in the hill region, dense forest, inaccessible or naturally isolated areas in Orissa. Even today, the large tribal population in the tribal belt continues to be rural. Lack of proper communication networks in these areas has failed to produce desirable results in various activities of tribal development in general and tribal education in particular. The tribal people who have suffered a lot from relative isolation for centuries, are not- popularly integrated with the mainstream of the Oriya society even today, and consequently suffer from backwardness, superstitions and other impediments of life. The teachers in tribal regions are found taking under advantages of their simplicity and ignorance. It is reported that in the tribal areas, the teachers indulge themselves in the consumption of liqueur. Even they are found sleeping during the school hours grossly violating their duties and responsibilities. Some of the teachers are actively involved in local politics and are engaged in petty business like many leading and contract works. Although higher officials and authorities are well aware of their fact, they do not take any action against them. The unholy alliance between the authority and the teachers blocks the educational development in the tribal areas.

In many cases, existence and functioning of Schools, midday meal programme, enrolment, attendance of students and teachers etc. are found only in the official records.

Tripathy & Padhy (2002) have examined the problem of education for tribal women. It has been observing that because of land alienation, poverty and lack of support system tribals in general and women in particular are in the web of misery, starvation and thus, leading, a sub-human living. Moreover, there is apathy of administrative personnel, lack of political will in implementing tribal programmes. It if further observed that there is large number of one-teacher schools in the interior tribal pockets. The teachers never attend the schools and the supervisor never supervises the schools. The teachers bribe the officials and \receive their salary in tribal belts of Orissa. The reality has not been reported in most cases. The important cause of high evidence of wastage and stagnation in tribal pockets of India are inadequate, insufficient and insincere role played by teacher appointed in tribal areas due to ineffective and corrupt administrative machinery.

Tripathy and Dash (2002) examined the role of tribal women in traditional crafts ad cottage industries. Collection of minor forest products like Sal leaf, bamboo, brown stick, etc. are largely performed by tribal women. The study concludes by stating, "It is highly imperative to develop the skill, knowledge and awareness among the tribals in general and tribal women in particular coupled with income generating labour intensive scheme in tribal regions through the development of agriculture infrastructure, household industries, crafts etc - which can bring about a catalytic change in their socio-economic conditions".

Dash and Mishra (2000) examined the role of forest resources in the development of tribals in several and tribal women in particular. He has pointed out that our people have changed the structure and function of forest eco-system in two fundamental ways. First, forest are utilised by the local population for their immediate needs. The methods applied span a range from ecological harmless gathering of non-Timber forest produces (NTFPs) such as fruits, barks, Flowers, leaves etc. as well as hunting to totally destructive modes of shifting cultivation. The socio-economic, cultural and religious impact of forest on human beings dwelling in and around it needs a special investigation, especially tribal women who are depending on forest since time immoral now faces the major problems before others realize it.

He suggested that the plight of tribal women can be arrested by protection and better management of forest resources as well as by planting more fruit bearing trees through a forestation programmes. Firmly relaxation for collection of NTFPs can not keep much as the tribals in general and tribe women in particular unable to secure proper value of their collection and processing due to (a) lack of marketing facility, (b) delay in Payment, (c) under valuation of NTFPs, (d) improper weight and measurement methods, (e) lack of knowledge (f) leasing the area of for procurement of NTFPs to a particular agency, has created single purchase market and restrict the optimum collection of NTFPs.

Panda (2000) highlighted the problem of migrant tribal female workers in urban informal sector. A host of factors are attributable for the migration of tribal female workers. Factors like insufficiency income at the place of origin, influence of friends & relatives, high-income possibility of the place of destination significantly determines the level of their migration.

Dr. Pasayat (2000) studied the factors responsible for ineffective participation of women in general and tribal women in particular in the process of democratic decentralisation through local bodies in the state of Orissa.

Dr. Behera and Mahanty (2000) reviewed the occupational structure and employment pattern of final women in Keonjhar district (Orissa).

Tribal women have the twin responsibilities of household management and supplementing family income through labour for wages. Various problems faced by them are heavy workload, irregular payment, lack of guarantee of work, lack of maternity benefits, health problems and absence of crèches facilities for children in the mining works. Economic compulsions pressurise the tribal children of tender age to work in many economic activities. Tribal agricultural labourers and other manual workers face the problem of lack of sufficiency work through out the year and victims of wage discrimination. Being needy, poor illiterate, ignorant and unorganised, they are almost at the mercy of the employers, middlemen and contractors.

Dr. Tripathy (2003) studied the impact of Development induced displacement on tribals. A number of commissions and committees were appointed from time to time to work into the problems of development in tribal regions of the country. These commissions suggested measures to remove the socio-economic imbalances and breakdown the psychological barrier that prevailed in the tribal pockets. But ironically, it has been observed that whenever river dam projects or industrialization process is embraced upon, the worst victims are tribals-who constitute significant segment of the total population of the project area.

Further, it has been observed that displacement of tribals in project area cause unfold misery as the life supporting system of tribals, the common property resources like land, forests etc. are snatched away from the tribals by the politicians, engineers and contractors. He has remarked that non-recognition of rights over resources and restrictions on their use, alienation of tribals from the means of production, denial of due entitlement of labour, distressed payments of wages and misappropriation of funds, thus, leakage of investible resources in tribal regions have kept the tribals in the web of misery and stagnation. In the tribal dominated states of India, the life supporting system of the local tribals have been snatched away by non-tribals and state institutions.

Dr. Panigrahi (2003) analyses the displacement and deprivation of tribal people in Orissa. Analyzing the impact of displacement on tribals he has stated that the youth dormitories, village Kothaghar named differently among different tribal communities no more remained as a source of renewing their moral and religious sanctions. The impersonal social gatherings are observed at liquor depose or at the tea stall. Gambling and cinema replace the traditional forms of recreation. This took them for away from their own traditions and customs.

The community festivals, which were very important for building their social organizations and for maintaining for social cohesion, have been broken down. The social distance maintained by boys & girls, married and unmarried has undergone changes. Among tribals the inter-ethnic marriages were more unthinkable in earlier days.

However, now cases of inter-ethnic marriages have been reported. The kith and kin that have exchanging their daughters in marriage among themselves were ceased to continue. The primary reasons for not giving daughters in marriage to the people of these household is that they will have no security, became there exists no lineage and clan no land and no forest for these groups. Displacement not only put them in problems in social spheres, but also brought about ecological hazard due to mining projects and industrial development.

Sen (2003) conducted a sample study in 8 villages (with in a radius of 15 kms.) inhabited by the Lanjia Saora. This study was sponsored by NABARD to review the status of the tribes and to find out the missing inputs so as to suggest corrective measures. The villages were located on the hills, deep inside the forests. The living conditions of tribals were miserable, while their non-tribal neighbours traders and middlemen were living a comfortable life despite the fact that they were not enjoying any rights on land and forest resources. It was found that in a different setting, where the tribals are progressive mind and organized, the situation was different.

The study further seeks to analyze the pathetic economic conditions of the tribal community in Orissa and the factors responsible for them. The author attributes this to the failure of government policies and programmes, the highbrow attitudes of academic institutions towards them and exploitation by the market forces.

The study highlighted that despite plethora of legislations, regulations and government orders to protect the tribals from exploitation, in the absence of adequate manpower those could not be made effective. The tribals are losing control over their land and assets. In several villages, the author met a number of families who migrated to distant places (Assam, Arunachal Pradesh, Maharastra, Gujarat etc.) for wage labour and spent about 6 - 8 months in a year. The middlemen (both Hindu and Christian) are exploiting the tribals, taking advantage of their ignorance about the existing legal and protective measures, cumbersome legal procedures and helplessness of the government machinery, which is ill equipped with funds and manpower. The study concluded that the NGOs, if are able to organize the poor tribals in informal/formal groups and mobilize the funds from financial institutions, the tribals will be able to create assets and resist exploitation, as a group.

As regards the measures for removal of backwardness the recommendations include the necessity of removing all types of exploitation from rural life and establish co-operatives on a planned basis- functional and regional, manned by proper persons who would work devotedly for the betterment of rural people.

According to the Committee on Social Welfare Team on Plan Projects (1959) commercial exploitation of forests is entrusted to the forest labourer's cooperatives rather than to contractors and thereby, the resulting profits are utilized for tribal welfare.

The Elwin Committee (1960) observed that of the many tribal problems, the greatest of all is poverty. The problem of indebtedness among the tribals is a major cause of their exploitation. The tribal borrowers are, therefore, 'born in debt, live in debt and pass away in debt'. The committee recommended saving the tribal people from poverty and fear and developing them along the line of their genius.

The Dhebar Commission (1961) recommended "the Sale and Marketing of the produce and supply of tribal people's requirements at reasonable price should receive special attention through cooperatives".

The Working Group on Cooperatives for Backward Classes (1961) attributed the slow development of cooperative movement in tribal areas to structural weakness, operational defects, management problems, faulty procedures and adoption of n=business methods and practices not suitable to tribals. The group suggested to separate organizational set up for promotion of cooperative movement among tribals so as to provide such services as were rendered by private traders and further recommended the formation of an "Integrated Cooperative" at Haat (Market) level.

The study team appointed by the Government of India (1971) to examine the cooperative structure in tribal development project areas under the chairmanship of Sri K.S. Bawa recommended organizational Large Sized Agricultural Multipurpose Cooperative Societies (LAMPS) in tribal areas to provide to the tribal members production as well as consumption credit, undertake marketing of agricultural and minor forest produce and distribute consumer necessaries as well as agricultural inputs so that the tribals could secure all facilities under one roof.

A review of literature on the Saoras reveals that no proper efforts have been made so far to properly understand their socio-cultural and economic lives so to have a proper perspective for their overall development. Nor much work has been done for the development of this tribe during pre-independence period.

In the light of the aforesaid studies it can be inferred that though a good deal of studies have been made on various issues of the tribals the intricate issue of socio- cultural aspects of tribals and most particularly the the soura tribe has not been explored.

It is only after independence of India that the Central as well as the State Government have launched some welfare programs and in the meantime some non-government organizations (NGOs) have initiated some programs for their development. To understand the socio -economic status of the Saoras in right perspective, it is necessary to have a complete view of their socio cultural and religious lives.

Therefore, an attempt has been in this paper to highlight briefly, the origin and history of Soura tribe, their habitat, demography, political system, kinship, marriage and their types, the characteristic features of Christian Saoras and Lanjia Saoras, the contact of Saoras with outsiders etc. Such a backdrop will acquaint the policy makers and researchers to adopt appropriate policy for the development of Saoras and Lanjia Saoras who mainly concentrate in Gajapati District.

Origin and History of Saoras

The very word 'Saoras' has been spelt and used in many ways. Regarding the origin of the Saoras reference materials can be found in ancient Sanskrit literature such as the Vedas, the epics, the purans and other religions texts.

According to a story mentioned in the *Aitreya Brahmana* of the *Rigveda* the Saoras are the descendants of the sons of Viswamitra, who were cursed to become impure and driven away by their father for an act of disobedience.

In the *Mahabharata* the tribes have been referred in several places. One such reference is the story of Nadini, the pet cow of the saint Vasishtta. The story goes that the king of Kanyakubja wanted to take possession of Nadini by paying the highest prices. However, Vasishtta declined to this offer. Then the king forcibly tried to take the cow, but to great wonder, the cow could protect herself by giving birth to so many groups of people from different parts of her body. It is believed that the Saoras came out from her dung.

In another story reference has been made to Jara Savara, who mistook Krishna for a deer and shot him with an arrow, which resulted in Krishna's death. In the Ramayan also there is a reference of Savari, a Saora woman whom Rama and Laxman met and partook her fruits while they were wondering in the Dandaka forests, looking for Sita.

The famous legend of Viswabasu, a Savara king, who had been worshipping Lord Jagannath in the forest for so many years till Indradyumna through Vidyapati duped him and tool over the Lord can also be included to study more about the Saora origin. Even the *Amarkosh*, a verse written in the 7th Century A.D. also keeps some records of the Saora tribe.

According to the verse like Nishada, Shwapacha, Kirqta, Pulinda and other primitive tribal people, the Saoras were also included in the list of Adibasi, the term used for the original inhabitants of India. These adibasis mostly settled down in the inaccessible hills and forest with hunting and food gathering as their occupation.

Some of the historical records seem to have references to the Saoras who once upon a time were powerful people, whether as kings as feudal chiefs.

General Cunningham (1879) records that Nandivarma Pallavamalla a Pallava King by name, claims to have released to hostile king of the Sabaras, Udayana, and captured his mirror-banner made of peacock's features (Thurston, 1993: 305).

Apart from the historical records there are some legends, which speak about the Saoras being the founders of some kingdoms in different parts of Orissa.

It is heard that a member of the Saora tribe named Dhenka Saora founded the erstwhile feudatory state of Dhenkanal. Another legend speaks about the founder of the Borasambar estate in Sambalpur state who was a crossbreed between a Rajput youth and a Lohara Saora girl. There are other legends also in different regions relating to the Saoras, which need some historical proofs.

The historical accounts relating to the origin of the Saoras do not enable us much to get a clear understanding of the ancient Saora tribe. However, one thing is clear that the Saoras are one of the most ancient settlers in Orissa. Being the most ancient tribe, the Saoras for centuries, have been living in the isolated hills and forests.

Habitat of Saoras

The Saoras are found to be inhabited amidst full of mountain ranges flanked by fertile valleys and plains. The Eastern Ghats, which traverses in north-south direction, keeps the compact Saora belt on its western side and the coastal plains in the eastern side Ganjam district.

As mentioned earlier, Parlakhemundi subdivision of Gajapati district is homeland of the Saoras. Adjacent of Parlakhemundi is the Gunpur subdivision of Koraput district, which lies to the west, is also lived by the Saoras. Particularly, in the villages around Gumma of Parlakhemundi subdivision and around Pottasingi of Gunupur subdivision are mostly inhabited by the Lamba Lanjia Saoras. These areas are generally inaccessible rising from two to three thousand feet and valleys radiate out in all directions.

There are also some small streams and rivulets for the tribals to get water for their different purposes such as bathing, washing clothes, etc. Thus, irrespective of all difficulties nature provides the tribal people various things they require for their livelihood from time to time.

The Saora habitat is thickly covered with vegetation Sal

(Shorea rubusta), the dominant specie found in the valleys. Among the other species are piasal (Pterocarpus Marsuplum) asane (Teminia Tomentosa), dharua (Phogeiesus latifolia), kusum (Carthamus Fictorus), harida (Terminalia Chebula), mohua (Madhuca Latifolia), amba (Mangifera indica), tentuli (Tamarindus indica), bahada (Terminalia belerica), amala (Phyllanthus emblica), gambhari (Gmelina arborea) etc. Some of the evergreen species such as, champa (Michelia champaca), karanja (Pongamia glabra), and baunsa (Dendorcalamus strictus) are common locally. A large number of medicinal plants are also available in the regions. Various flowering creepers and grasses are also found such as sialilata (Bauxinia vahlli), sabai (Imperrata arundinacea) etc.

The fauna of the areas are elephants (Elophas maximums indicus), tigers (Panther-tigers), leopards (Panthera pardus), wild dogs (Cuon alpinus), jackals (canis aureus), foxes (Vulpses bengalensis), black bears (Melursus ursinus), wild bears (Sua acrofa oristtus, wagner), sambars (Carvus unicolor olgar, Blainville muntjak), spotted deers (Axis axis), barking deers (Muntiacus), nilgais (Boselaphus tragocamelus), antelopes (Tetracerus quadricornis), etc. Birds of hetrogenous type with their beautiful plumage are also noticeable.

The birds found in the forests include peafowl, peacock, red jungle fowl, mayna, etc. Different kinds of reptiles such as godhi, chameleons and different species of snakes are found in the area.

Anthropologists have been fascinated at the beautiful sights of the Saoras living. Writing about the Saora habitat N.Patnaik (1989, p.8) thus, describes:

> On the whole, the Saoras habitat is a lovely country with rolling mountains, undulating meadows, roaring rapids and enchanting water falls, terraced fields, varied flora and fauna. Likewise the Saoras with their colorful costumes and adornments, enchanting music accompanied by dancing in which both men and women participate and which speak of their spontaneous display of joyous life, provide an example of a tribe living in comparative freedom and in close relationship with nature.

Demography

Saora population in Orissa, according to 1981 census, is 3, 70,060. The distribution of Saora population in thirteen undivided districts of Orissa is depicted in Table 4.1

Table 4.1
Distribution of Saora population in the undivided districts of Orissa (in number)

Name of the undivided districts	ST Population	Saora Population	% of Saora ST Population
Sambalpur	6,20,555	1,07,697	17.35
Ganjam	4,53,934	69,201	17.34
Bolangir	2,80,381	46,587	16.61
Koraput	13,71,550	45,941	3.34
Puri	1,00,827	35,418	35.12
Cuttack	1,44,708	22,019	15.21
Dhenkanal	1,94,060	20,298	10.45
Keonjhar	4,99,567	7,929	1.58
Kalahandi	4,18,871	5,695	1.35
Phulbani	2,79,276	3,363	1.20
Mayurbhanj	9,12,320	2,903	0.31
Balasor	1,54,153	1,622	1.05
Sundargarh	6,85,765	1,388	0.20

Source: 1981 Census, Govt. of India.

It is seen from the Table 4.1 that in five districts such as Sambalpur, Ganjam, Bolangir, Koraput and Puri population of the Saoras is above 30,000 in each district. Percentage of the Saora population against the total population of the tribals in the above five districts varied between 3.34 to 35.12 per cent. Though in Koraput the Saoras are significant in number (45, 941) their percentage against the percentage of total tribal population is less (3.34 per cent). However, in Puri district the population of the Saoras is only 35, 418 while their percentage against the total tribal population is more than 35 per cent.

In the districts of Dhenkanal and Cuttack the Saora population is little over 20,000 (20,298 and 22, 019) while their percentage against total tribal population of these districts are 10.45 and 15.27 per cent respectively.

Further, from Table 4.2 it is observed that the female population of Saoras in comparison to male population is more in all districts of Orissa except Cuttack, Keonjhar, Kalahandi and Balasore.

Table 4.2

Distribution of Saora population in the undivided districts of Orissa on the basis of sex (in number) as per 1981 census

Name of the undivided districts	Male	%	Female	%	Total	Female per 1000 male
Sambalpur	5,3105	49.31	5,4592	50.69	1,07,697	1028
Ganjam	3,3632	48	3,5569	51.40	69,201	1057
Bolangir	2,2929	60	2,3657	50.78	46,586	1032
Koraput	2,2584	49.16	2,3356	50.84	45,940	1034
Puri	1,7483	49.36	1,7936	50.64	35,418	1026
Cuttack	1,1029	50.08	1,0990	49.91	22,019	996
Dhenkanal	1,0112	49.82	1,0186	50.18	20,298	1007
Keonjhar	3989	50.31	3940	49.69	7,929	988
Kalahandi	2876	50.49	2820	49.51	5,696	980
Phulbani	1664	49.49	1696	50.50	3,362	1019
Mayurbhanj	1440	49.60	1463	50.40	2,903	1016
Balasore	818	50.43	804	49.57	1,622	983
Sundargarh	683	49.21	705	50.79	1,388	1032
Total	1,82,344		1,87,716		3,70,060	

Source: 1981 Census, Govt. of India

Besides Orissa, some of the bordering States have significant number of the Saora population, which is evident from Table 4.3. It is clear that the state, Orissa has the largest number of Saora Population in comparison to its neighboring states like Andhra Pradesh, Madhya Pradesh, West Bengal and Bihar.

Table 4.3

Distribution of Saora population in Orissa and neighbouring states

Sl. No.	Name of the state	Name of the Tribe	Number
1	Orissa	Saora	3,70,060
2	Andhra Pradesh	Saora	82,101
3	Madhya Pradesh	Savar	63,773
4	West Bengal	Savar	37,297
5	Bihar	Savar	3,014

Source: 1981 Census, Govt. of India.

Classification

The Saora tribe is divided into several subdivisions mainly based on differences in their occupation and culture. Thurston (1993) broadly divides the Saoras into two categories, i.e., (i) Hill Savaras and (ii) Savaras of the low country. The main subdivisions of the Saoras can be listed as in the following:

1. Lamba Lanjia Saoras
2. Jadu Saoras
3. Mane Saoras
4. Raika Saoras
5. Sarada Saoras
6. Kindol Saoras
7. Arsi Saoras
8. Juari Saoras
9. Kancher Saoras
10. Kurumba Saoras
11. Sudha Saoras
12. Jati Saoras
13. Jara Saoras
14. Bhima Saoras and
15. Kampo Saoras

The Lamba Lanjia Saoras are mostly found in Paralakhemundi subdivision of Gajapati district and Pottasingi area of Gunpur Taluk in Koraput district. The Langia Saora group has got special significance in the sense that the male members of the group hung down their loin clothes, which look like long tails. Thus,

Lamba Lanjia Saora meaning there by long-tailed Saora. By occupation the Lamba Lanjia Saoras are mainly shifting cultivators. They also weave the coarse clothes worn either by members of the tribe or the Scheduled Caste and other which include agricultural labourers. Comparing to other sections of the Saoras the Lamba Lanjia Saoras are the least developed groups.

The Jadu Saoras who live in Bada Khemundi area of Ganjam district by nature do not worship the cow as Gomata as some of their fellow group does. Instead thy eat beef. The Mane Saoras are mostly found in Ajoygoda Mutha in the Ganjam district and they work on brass. The Raika Saoras who inhabit in Rayagarha Mutha and other parts of Parlakhemundi subdivision abstain from eating animal flesh.

The Kondol Saoras who are also known as Tankla Saoras are experts in basket making. The Arsi Saoras like the Lamba Lanjia Saoras are by profession a weaving group who also eat beef. The Juari Saoras are skilled in cutting date palms. The Kandchers are seemed to be good archers and the Kurumbas are primarily shifting cultivators.

The Sudha and the Jati Saoras pose themselves as forward and more civilized comparing to the other sections of the tribe. The main occupation of both these groups in shifting cultivation and they speak Oriya language. On the other hand, the Kampo Saoras speak in Telugu language.

It is known that while the Kampo Saoras have retained many of ancient Saora customs, the Sudha Saoras, in the meantime, have adopted the language and customs of the Oriya people. The Kampos are also sometimes called Kudunga or Baseng. G.V. Ramamurti, the authority on the Saoras believes that the term 'Baseng' has been derived from the Saora word 'basi', which means 'salt'.

Ramamurti states that the term Baseng is applied to the plains below the ghats where the fairs are held and there salt is purchased by the Saoras of the hills, and the name used to designate the Saoras living there. Ramamurti also writes that the name Kampo implies that "the Savaras of this class have adopted the customs of the Hindu Kampus (Oriya for Kaput), Kurumba is another name by which they are known, but it is reported that there is a subdivision of them called by this name" (Thurston: 1993, p.309).

The Jara Saoras claim their ancestry to Jara Savara, who is believed to have killed Krishna with his arrow. The Bhima Saoras who live in Jirang area of Gajapati district trace their association with Bhima, one of the five Pandavas described in the Mahabharat. They worship Hindu Gods and Goddesses as well. The Kurumba Saoras are basically potters who make earthen pots. In connection with the pots made by the Kurumbas Fawcett thus writes, "These pots are made in a few villages in the Saora hills. Earthen vessels are used for cooking or for hanging up in houses as fetishes of ancestral spirits of certain deities".

Saora sub-groups and their languages

With regard to the physical features of the Saoras of Orissa, Fawcett describes thus: "below the middle height; face rather flat; lips thick; nose broad and flat; check bones high; eyes slightly oblique. They are as fair as the Uriyas, and fairer than the Telugus of the plains. Not only is the Saora shorter and fairer than other hill people, but his face is distinctly Mongolian, the obliquity of the eyes being sometimes very marked, and the inner corners of the eyes are generally very oblique".

Thus, this description of the Saoras gives a picture that their racial affinity is with Mongolide group. But an anthropologist like N.Patnaik (1989) suggests that the Saoras of Orissa are belonged to the Proto-Australoid family. The language of the Saoras is called Sora, which belongs to the south Munda branch of Austric language family (N.Patnaik 1989, p.1).

G.A Grierson, a pioneer in the fields of tribal language and culture include the Saora language in the munda family in 1906. Grierson observes that the Saora language has become a mixed language in the meantime with largely influenced by Telugu. He also points out that the Saora language has some affinities with Kharia and Juang languages as well.

However, V.Elwin in his classic book titled 'Religion of an Indian Tribe' opines that though the Saora language has some affinities with Kharia and Juang languages it is closely allied to the Gutob and Pareng languages. He does not agree with Grierson that the Saora language has been diluted too much by admixture. He rather suggests that the language of the hills is remarkable pure and has become rich by giving space to a few Telugu and Oriya words. Elwin is right to the extent that great majority of the hill Saoras now also speak in their original chaste language. But, it cannot be generalized by saying that all the Saoras do the same allover Orissa.

G.V. Ramamurti, an expert on the Saora language thus writes that, "The language-speaking among the Saora varies considerably not only between villages but also between individuals". This observation has been found correct during field studies in Gumma block Parlakhemundi Subdivisions of Gajapati district to study about various aspects of the Saoras.

Political System of Saora Villages

Leadership among the Saoras is of two kinds as it is seen in other tribal communities also. They are (i) Social/Political head and (ii) Religious ahead. Gomang is the Social/Political head, while Buryya is the religious leader. The word Gomang means a great person.

Along with the Gomang the Buyya has also the same power of a magistrate. Apart from the political decisions, these two leaders have complete right on religious matters as well. Thus, in every village the people are under the control of these two leaders.

Apart from these important offices some villages have the post of Disari, who act as an astrologer. This post is not ascribed but is achieved by seer deeds. The man who acquires requisite knowledge about starts becomes an astrologer. There is also a post of Barik seen in most villages. The basic duty of the Barik is to carry the messages from one village to another.

The offices of the Gomang and the Buyyan function on hereditary basis. Generally the eldest son has the right to succeed to the office but in case he does not have necessary qualities and experiences the post naturally goes to the younger son. But for the Buyya it is not just hereditary right, what is important is, the person who will inherit the post should have a sound knowledge of the religious customs and practices of the Saora community.

The Gomang and the Buyya attend in each and every occasion of the community affairs such as marriage, funeral and other festivals of the village. Matter relating to purchase, sale and mortgage of land, trees or other things are also decided by these two, of course, with the prior opinions of elderly members of the community.

Since these two have also certain executive powers, they decide over certain criminal cases as well. Ordinarily, for any common offences, the accused has to pay some fine, may be, two pots of liquor and one goat or he/she has to feed the entire village members. The exact quantity of fine is decided considering the gravity of the offence.

It was during the British rule in Orissa that the self-government system of the Saoras and also the other tribals came to an end. During the British rule the hill tracts of undivided Ganjam was under some hill chiefs. Each hill-tract called maliah was divided into a number of administrative subdivisions known that time as Mathas. Each Matha was under a Matha head called Bissoyi or Patra. Each Bishoyi used to maintain a number of hereditary officers such as Adhikari, Muddadars, Paiks and Naiks stationed at the different headquarters and strategic places of the Mathas.

At the village Matha there were few official employed by the Bissoyi for collecting revenue from the villagers. Thus, it is in this connection that Gomang post was created who would be responsible for paying land-revenue to the Government. Apart from the Gomang the British Government also recognised the important roles of Barik (mediator), Beju (worshipper) Behera (carrier).

Mandia (watchman) is meant for the smooth functioning of the village administration. Thus, it can be said that the entire system was feudal in character with the Zamindar, Muthadar and Gomang forming the hierarchy in descending order in the past and ruling over the tribal subjects.

Thus, with the introduction of a hierarchical administrative setup during the British rule, the Pachayat system of the Saoras, which stood for people's democracy, lost its tradition.

Kinship and Marriage

Kinship: It is interesting to note that the Saoras and having no clan or sib organisation. Their main exogamous unit is the extended family descended from the common ancestor, which is called Birinda. Marriage is strictly prohibited within a birinda as the members of birinda treat each other as brothers. As a matter of solidarity and fraternity all the members of a birinda must meet during the Guar (second death ceremony).

In case of a member of the birinda is issueless and no heir is there to inherit the property then it is the birinda to inherit the same. It is basically a patrilineage system, the women even after their marriage identify themselves their father's birinda. Members of a birinda are seen living in one village or surrounded areas of one villager and their membership to the birinda remain the same as earlier as the bones etc of the dead persons are collected and brought to the original village for the final rites. Thus, the birinda phenomenon can be compared with Hindu concept of Sapinda.

Family is the small social unit among the Saoras. The Saoras family is mostly a nuclear one comprising of married couple and their unmarried off springs. Sometimes, of course, there compound families in case there is more then one wife in the house. But in that case, there will be separate house for each of the wife and her children.

There are few extended families having parents and their married sons and grand children living together. Rarely one can find join families with several married brothers staying together.

The size of the Saora family is usually small consisting of four to six members. The residence is patrilocal and hence the descent is patrilineal. The membership in the Saora family is acquired by birth, but girls after their marriage leave parent's family and stay with their husbands. Taking part in all economic activities, living in a common residence and cooking and eating together are common features in each and every Saoras family. That's why some denotative terms are being used by the Saoras among their primary relatives and these are rarely being used among the secondary relatives.

Some of the denominal terms found among the Saoras are

compared with general Oriyas and their translation in English have been depicted in the Table 4.4.

Table 4.4

Translation of some Saora terms into Oriya and English

Saora term	Oriya	English
Wang	Bapa	Father
Yang	Maa	Mother
Obang	Bhai	Brother
Aying	Bhauni	Sister
Mandrayen	Swami	Husband
Ansalayan/Dukri	Stree	Wife
Kinar	Sasu	Mother-in-law
Kunar	Sasura	Father-in-law
Anger	Pua	Son
Ansedaon	Jhia	Daughter
Uleng	Nati	Grand Son
Uleng	Natuni	Grand Daughter
Jujang	Jeje	Grand Father
Yagung	Jejma	Grand Mother
Dadi	Kaka	Uncle
Awamg	Pieesi	Aunt
Jujung	Aja	Mother's Father
Yayung	Aee	Mother
Eris	Diara	Husband's Brother
Alibai	Nananda	Husband's Sister
Eris	Sala	Wife's Brother
Alibai	Sali	Wife's Sister
Rayam	Nanadei	Husband's Sister's Husband
Kakan	Badaja	Husband's Brother's Wife
Kayin	Sanaja	-do-

Marriage System of Saoras

Regarding the marriage customs of the Saoras Mr. Fawcett has been quoted extensively in Thurston and Rangachri's "Caster and Tribe of Southern India, a Saora may marry a woman of his own or of any other village. A man may have as many as three wives or, if he is man of importance, such as Gomango of large village, he may have four. Not that there is any law in the matter, but it is considered that there or at most four, are as many as man can manage. For his first marriage, a man chooses a young woman.

A woman may leave her husband whenever she pleases. He husband cannot prevent her. When a woman leaves her husband to join herself to another, the other pays the husband she has left a buffalo and a pig. Formerly, it is said that, it he did not pay up, the man she left would kill the man to whom she went. Now arbitration comes into play. As getting of the first wife is more troublesome and expensive than getting the other, she is treated the best. In some places, a man's all wives are said to live together peaceably..."

In the past the Saoras used to observe village exogamy because the village was comprised of one lineage. In recent years the village composition has become multi -linear. Therefore, occurrence of inter village marriage is not uncommon among the Saoras. As mentioned earlier a woman of the Saoras community does not change her birinda even after her marriage.

In this context father's sister being a member of the same birinda, it is not possible to marry with her children. Only those who fail to arrange girls for their sons elsewhere may be forced to select one of the maternal cross cousins (mother's brother's daughter) for marriage. There is as such no particular age fixed for the marriage of the boys and girls.

Both child and adult marriages are seen taking place among the Saoras. It is found that premarital relation is not taken as a serious offence in the society. If a girl prior to her marriage becomes pregnant or had some abortions, nobody takes serious note of it. It may be because there is no difficulty in finding a boy for her. In fact, in most of such cases, the person who is responsible for the pregnancy normally marries the girl. Although polygamy is allowed polyandry is not encouraged in the Saoras society.

Types of Marriage

There are different forms of marriage prevailed among the Saoras. The noted three kinds of marriage are Marriage by arrangement, Marriage by capture and marriage by service. Apart from these, there are also remarriage of windows and divorcees, which have also important bearing on the Saora society.

Marriage by arrangement is the most common form of marriage among the Saoras. Parents and relatives of the groom who take initiative basically make the arrangements. The father of the boy along with his relatives takes the proposal to the girl's house taking a pot of wine. The custom is that he offers the liquor pots to the parents of the girl and proposes by saying, "can you offer the sweetest flower in your garden, the scent of which we have smelled form such a long distance?" The parents of the girl then discusses about the proposal among their kinsmen. The opinion of the girl is also sought. If they agree with the proposal, the pot of wine brought by the boy's relatives is accepted and distributed among the relatives and close friends of both the parties. This is the first step of the arranged marriage.

Once the proposal is accepted there are several visiting to the girl's sides by the boy's relatives. Every time they visit they carry one or more pots of wine. During one of such visits an arrow is given to the girl's side and engagement is fixed then. In another visit these two parties sit and finalize about the amount and nature of the bride price.

Generally bride price is collected in the form of cash, grains, liquor, etc. The amount of bride price among the Saoras is Rs. 100/- either along with or sometimes exclusively of 20 pots of wine, 15 kg. of rice, 20 kg. of paddy, 9 bangles and a saree for the mother of the bride. Betrothal takes place in an appointed day with the groom visiting the bride's house. Most of the family members, friends and other relatives attend the ceremony and take part in dance, drinking and eating. A big feast is prepared for all by killing a goat, pig or even a buffalo. During the betrothal ceremony no priest or shaman is required to formalize the celebration. Only the wind is being offered to the ancestors before it is drunk. On the same night the bride is brought to the boy's house.

The second kind of marriage i.e., marriage by force/capture otherwise known as Danda Boi, is not commonly prevalent among the Saoras. The Saoras despise for this form of marriage but sometime it occurs among them. The practice of this form of marriage is that a young man takes a fancy for a girl of another village. He informs this thing to his friends and all of them are on the look out for an opportunity to kidnap the girl. All of them either individually or collectively watch her movements always searching for convenient opportunity.

When the girl goes to a work place, market or for a visit, the young man goes stealthy and catches her by arms. Immediately his companions catch hold of and drag her towards their village. If the villagers see them immediately they will be retaliated with lathies and other weapons. If the kidnapping is not interfered with, the girl is left at house of the young man. She is persuaded by the villagers to agree to marry the young man. If the girl does not agree there is a complaint made to Mutha Head. Suitable compensation is given according to changes made by the Mutha. If the girl agrees the boy has to give a feast to the community plus adequate compensation for the parents.

In the Saora community widow is generally allowed to remarry. The young brother of the deceased is the immediate choice. If he does not agree, she tries for an outsider. But then the rule is, one should not take out any household articles or any property from her deceased husband's house.

Her new husband offers a buffalo or a pig to her brother-in-law which is offered for the dead man's spirit by the shaman who prays: "I am offering this meal and drink to you and with this the previous relationship between you and the woman ceases and she is not taking any article or property with her. The woman should not be troubled either in the house or in the hill or forest or when asleep or when awake. The person who is not marrying her did not cause any harm to you. She liked him and desired the marring her did not cause any harm to you. She liked him and desired the marriage. Thereupon, only he agreed to marry her. Please take these and be satisfied. All you ancestors are witnesses of this solemn prayer and you should abide by it." Thus, the marriage is completed over a feast.

It is interesting to note that a Saora can marry a stepmother after his father's death. This remarriage is called yayangkoi. This possible only when the son is quite a grown up and wife of the deceased one is young.

The tradition of this kind of marriage is based on their belief pattern. The Saoras are on the belief that the deceased father admonishes the son in dreams and threatens upon the consequences if he fails in his duty to marry his stepmother. The son then buys a buffalo, two bangles and a new cloth. The buffalo is ceremoniously sacrificed and offered to the decreased.

In the ceremony one of the bangles is put in the son's hand and the other into the hand of the woman. This ceremony is followed by a feast with wine and meat, which is enjoyed by all the members of the birinda and other friends and relations. The entire ceremony is a process of social approval accorded to the stepmother and the stepson who become wife and husband and live together.

Divorce among the Saoras is not uncommon though; it is generally not very much prevalent. If a husband is not able to satisfy his wife with sexual pleasure on account of impotency or when he refuses to build up an independent house even if she pressurizes and when the wife quarrels with her sisters-in-law, in this situations a wife can automatically leave her husband. On the other hand if the wife is unfaithful or known to behaving clandestine affairs with others or ill-treating children then the husband can desert her. In the case of the wife remarrying, the former husband collects compensation from the new husband. But when the husband forcibly deserts her the wife can complain to Gomang so that the compensation payable at the time of remarriage is reduced.

The present Saora religion is a mixture of both Hinduism and Christianity along with some of the traditional customs and conventions incorporated into it. In spite of all these changes no disharmony is found in the area and people are seen living peacefully respecting each other's religion. Some of the common behaviour pattern of the Saoras following Christianity and Hinduism are as follows:

Christian Saoras

1. Visit Church on Sunday and other important occasions connected with Church.

2. Attend traditional festivals connected with agricultural operation (sowing of seeds, harvesting) visit church and offer cereals and cash for joint feast.

3. During marriage and betrothal ceremony, visit Church along with few relatives and offer cash or kind to the Church as well as the priest.

4. Display paintings and photographs of Christ or holy cross on the wall facing the door.

5. Besides church, there is no sacred place in the village. Those who can read Roman script have been provided with a copy of the Bible translated in Saora language.

6. In the Church there is hierarchy. The chief priest is known as Palak, under whom there are two Dikons. The Dikons are assisted by Chalaks. All these functional look after the need of the tribals living in the surrounding villages.

7. While observing rituals animal sacrifice is not encouraged. However, since all major ceremonies are followed with common feasts, animal sacrifices are made in a separate place. Liquor is not offered in the Church for the guests.

Hindus Saoras

1. Visit temple if located in the village during the festivals connected with Hindu religion.

2. Attend traditional festivals and important rituals connected with Hindu Gods and Goddess and agricultural operations (both sowing and harvesting), visit temples and offer cereals and cash for joint feast.

3. Normally marriage, name giving and death rituals/ceremonies are held at house. The priest is invited for conducting the rituals and the priest is offered cash and some food for the services rendered.

4. Display photographs of Gods and Goddesses like Shiva, Jagannath, Ganesh, Durga, Kali, Laxmi etc. on the wall near the entrance.

5. Since no Hindu scripture have been translated in Saora language, the tribals are not able to understand the philosophy and richness of the religious thoughts and behavior.

6. The priests, if available, can be called to visit the residence of the individual or be present at the temple to perform the specific rituals. No specific effort is made by the priest to solve the problems of the tribals and provide relief.

7. Mostly animal sacrifices are made. However, buffalo or cow is not sacrificed. Non-vegetarian food is an integral part of the ceremonies and rituals. Liquor is also offered to the Gods and Goddesses. Younger generation is giving up the habits of smoking and drinking. Eating of beef is prohibited.

8. It is seen that the Hindu or the Christian Saoras enjoy higher status comparing to the Saoras who are still untouched by the forces of modernization. The Christian Saoras are comparatively educated since the missionaries make education facilities available to them. Otherwise, also voluntary workers motivate the Saoras to avail education facilities.

It has been observed that the educated Saoras whether Christians or Hindus develop clean habits, become conscious about various preventive measures for better health status, aware of about the bad effects of liquor and smoking etc.

Both the Hindus and Christian Saoras have in the meantime discarded those traditional rituals connected with death and marriage, which were expensive and time consuming. Animal sacrifice, feast, liquor etc. during the various ceremonies are gradually being discouraged. The Hindu converts are in favor of non-vegetarian foodstuff. The Christian Saoras have started attending the church on Sundays and other festive occasions, where they meet with each other, exchange good wished, discuss about emerging problems and contribute for the feast arranged in those occasions so that no one feels burdened for such gatherings.

The Church has become the forum for dissemination of information about new development schemes, policies of the government and how best those schemes can be implemented. Activities like awareness camps, motivation, skill formation and distribution of assets are being arranged in the Church premises.

Relationship with the neighbors and outsiders

Barring some inaccessible hills and valleys, people of different castes and tribes live alongside the Saoras. Anthropologists view the relationships between the neighbouring castes, tribes and Saoras in two different ways: Symbiotic as well as exploitative. Generally the following groups are found to be neighbors of the Saoras.

The relationship with Panos

Panos are, perhaps the only group who are very close to the Saoras. They are one of the Scheduled Caste communities whose traditional occupation is weaving cloths, basket making, drum beating etc. They do some pretty business supplying necessary goods, such as salt, tobacco, dry fish, clothes, etc. to the Saoras. The Panos also supply sacrificing animals and birds for various rituals observed by the Saoras from time to time. On the return of the services the Saoras pay them in kinds. The Panos join in various socio-cultural and religious programs, which bring them close proximity with the Saoras. This is a symbiotic relationship. However, some anthropologists opine that the Panos exploit innocent Saoras in various ways and depict them in negative light. They explain that originally the Panos are weavers by profession and supply the Saoras with the clothes that the latter need. In course of time, however, the Panos have started pretty money lending business and become middlemen between the hill folk and plain people. The Panos, on account of their contacts with the outside world, a relatively higher percentage of literacy compared to the tribals and conversion to Christianity etc. seemed to be clever and witty people, the anthropologist's remark. They cite the example that the Panos take away the agricultural and minor forest produce of the Saoras for small consideration and sell it in high prices in nearby towns. This the Panos do, the anthropologist believe, by exploiting the psychological state of the tribals, requiring funds to perform an animal sacrifice to drive away illness or other religious ceremonies.

However, many anthropologists do not agree to the view that the Panos are the exploiters of the Saoras: rather the Panos are inevitably the most desired friends of the Saoras, they say. Studying the social interrelationship between the Saoras and the Panos of Ganjam agency Nityananda Das (1989) thus writes:

> The Pano-Saora relationship is not one of the parasitism but symbiosis. (The) Panos help (the) Saoras during the lean months. They bring various articles to the doorsteps of (the) Saoras and also advance credit on oral promise to pay back. Old and infirm animals are exchanged. More necessities of life like salt, tobacco, dry fish, and clothes are freely advanced.

Our analysis is that the later view is correct. The Pano is a friend, philosopher and guide of the Saora. The Panos according to our survey are poorer than the Saoras. They are land less, asset less and engage themselves as agricultural labourers and wage earners in the field and land of the Saoras.

The relationship with Goudas

The Goudas are the herders or milkmen cast people who have very intimate relationship with the Saoras, the herders basically supply draft cattle on loan basis and thereby the Saoras can supplement their draft animals at the time of agricultural works. Besides this, the Saoras request the herders to take care of their cattle during the summer season so that the cattle get some nutrition. Apart from the agricultural works, there is also social interaction between the Saoras and the Goudas.

Relationship with Oriyas

The Saoras refer to the upper castes, especially the Paikas and Khandayats as Oriyas. It is heard from the Saoras that the caste people were earlier exploiting them in many ways, which also continues even till to day in various forms. Most of the upper caste people are basically migrants who are pretty government serpents, businessmen by profession in the tribal areas. Thus, both the groups interact with each other and try to maintain cordial relationship.

The Saoras also occasionally get some services from other caste people. For example, the Hinis, another Scheduled Caste (Panos and Dombs) community people come to the Saora villages with their bamboo basket and winnowing fans, for selling, earlier they were receiving their payment in kinds, but nowadays, they are paid in cash. They mostly come during harvesting season. Potters are also frequently seen in the Saora villages during harvesting season. They come from distant villages to sell their product, either through barter or money. They sometimes spend the night in the village if they are late and generally sleep at the varandah of the village headman or Gomang. The others who are seen visiting the villages are paddlers, beggars, sanyasis, snake charmers, magicians, etc.

Contact with outside institutions

Mostly after India's independence both Central as well as State Government have taken several measures to improve the living standard of the Saoras in many ways. To bring different tribal programmes into action, Government of Orissa has set up some Tribal Development Blocks (TD) in the sixties of this century. Since the beginning of the Fifth Five Year Plan special attention has been taken for the overall improvement of some of the primitive tribes, the Saoras being one, under the Integrated Tribal Development Agency (ITDA). Under this programme the Lanjia Saora Development Agency (LSDA) has been established at Serango in 1979, which comes under the Gumma Block of newly formed Gajapati district. It may be mentioned here that the primitive tribes are identified on the basis of their diminishing population, traditional economy, isolation and so on. The thrust areas of development are agriculture, horticulture, soil conservation and animal husbandry. In addition to these the provision of drinking water supply, education and health is also taken up which are the minimum basic needs for the Saoras.

The LSDA at Serango functions under the supervision of the Integrated Tribal Development Agency, Parlakhemundi which is the nodal agency in terms of plan formulation, implementation of programmes and to give operational effect to the Tribal sub-plan concept.

According to a report of the Integrated Tribal Development Agency, Paralakhemundi, against the target of 1830 Scheduled Tribe families for 1993-94, 5149 families have been assisted for different programmes, such as irrigation, plantation, land development, beekeeping, tailoring etc.

For their health and medicine, the Saoras mostly depend on the Christian hospital located at Serango. It is a well-equipped hospital with adequate manpower. Recently the hospital has been expanded. Apart from the treatment of the common disease like fever, cold malaria, serious ailments and diseases are also treated there. A cabin costing Rs. 300 per day is available for the patient. The rate appears to be cheap for an outsider but for the Saoras this is quite expensive. According to hospital authorities micro-surgery has recently been started and there may be much more expansion of it in near future.

There is another Health sub-centre at Serango and a Primary Health Centre (PHC) near the block office at Gumma. Compared to the Chriestian hospital mentioned-above. Facilities available in these two Health centres appear to be inadequate. Most of the Saoras prefer to the Christian hospital. Serious ailments are referred to the Government hospital at Paralakhemundi.

Apart from these institution mentioned above, there are also some Ashram schools, Churches in and around Gumma Block and their day to day functions, some way or other have impact on the Saora lives.

Conclusion

It is inferred from the foregoing analysis that the genesis of Soura tribe has been deeply rooted in antiquity. Existence of Soura tribe has its mention in Vedas, Mahabharata and Ramayan. They are presently found in Gunpur sub-division of undivided Koraput and Paralakhemundi subdivision of Gajapati district. There are 15 types of Saoras found in Orissa and other states.

There is a distinctive political system manifested in the Soura villages. There are also difference forms of marriages found among the Saoras.

The socio-cultural aspects of Saoras reveal some interesting teachers regarding their kinship, language, customs, traditions and their relationship with other caste people and outsiders. There are some differences between Christian Saoras and Hindu Saoras.

The Lanjia Saoras are the most backward primitive tribals from among the different types of Saoras. The LSDA has made specific efforts to ameliorate the socio-economic conditions of Langia Soura tribals.

NOTES

1. According to Skanda Purana (Utkala Khanda) Lord Vishnu (Nilmadhava) was being worshipped by the Sabara tribals. Lord Jagannath was a tribal deity (form of a Daru i.e. sacred tree). The legends mentioned in Brahma Purana states that the Sabaras of Malkangiri area were worshippers of the Sthanumurti (a branchless tree trunk), which is course of time, replaced the primitive tree worship.

2. The fifteen-century tradition Jagannath resembles the log of wood as spoken of in the Sruti. The Sabaras worshipped a deity named Kitnung whop had ten synonyms and one of the synonyms was jaganta or Jaganelo.

3. An interesting tradition recorded in the Vizagpatnam plates (AD 1119) reveals that King Kamarnave conqurred the Mahendragiri region towards the close of the fifth century A.D acknowledge a tribal deity of the Sabara tribe as Siva Gokarneswar and worshipped it as the tutelary deity (ista devta) of the family. According to the traditional followed in the Jagannath temple during Navakelebar the Patimahapatra (head of the half Savara Brahmins and the decedents of Brahmin Vidyapati and the Savara Lalita) who leads the party of the Daitas (temple priests) to find out the Daru (sacred tree) for the four deities, is informed about the exact location of the Darus. The rituals connected with Stambheswari (tribal Deity) Devi closely resembled with the Navakalebara of Lord Jagannath.

4. The Daitas (descendants of Soura Chief) special group of priests play significant role in the worship of Lord Jagannath. The Aryan invaders who settled amidst the tribes, in course of time adopted and worshipped some tribal Gods and Goddesses and they were raised in course of time.

During Muslim invasion some of the Hindu rulers migrated to the hills for safety and finally settled in the hills. The Hindu rulers and kings donated rent-free villagers/landing the remote areas to selected persons/representatives to look after the administration of those areas and provide necessary services to the rulers. Those representatives came in contact with the local tribals and interaction took place between the tribals and the non-tribals who were Hindus. This assimilation process blended the tribal religion and the Hindu religion into a mixed religion, each having influence of the others.

The Goddesses Stambheswari (Khambeswari) Vyaghradevi and Tara-Tarini are examples of aboriginal cult Goddesses of the Ganjam district, which under went the process of Aryanisation. These deities have no specific iconographic features and they do not find mention in the Brahminical theology. Those were worshipped in the form of stone or tree trunks, kept in the open space (on hill tops or forests or one corner of the settlement) and gradually given a shelter within a structure. Animal sacrifices were a must and human sacrifices (in the past) on specific occasions were not uncommon.

In some temples the stone images have been given some form or shape while in front of such temples wooden poles or stone pillars were being worshipped which retained aboriginal character in the form of crude carvings (B.C.Roy, 1989, New Delhi, P-129).

5

Provision of Employment and Right to Work*

When large number of able-bodied persons of working age willing to work but do not find employment in the prevailing wage rate, they are termed as unemployed.

As basic means of livelihood, provision of employment has been the crucial policy perspective of the central and state governments. It was conceived in that realization of economic growth would automatically promote employment and improve the quality of life. But later on it was felt that provision of employment for poor would generate employment. The acute problem of unemployment and underemployment in rural areas has resulted in abject poverty. Hence, an integral approach to economic development and poverty reduction must encompass employment growth, social security, education and health. Therefore, supplementary employment avenues have been provided in our country through wage employment programmes with a view to alleviating the poverty.

A plethora of employment generating programmes have been initiated in our country since 1970's with the objective of strengthening the rural infrastructure, creating community assets and finally, eradicating the poverty in the rural areas.

*Paper presented in the 47th Annual Conference of the Indian Society of Labour Economics, held at JNU, New Delhi on 16th December, 2005.

In the year 1989-90, Jawahar Rozgar Yojana (JRY) was introduced after the merger of National Rural Employment Programme and Rural Landless Employment Guarantee Programme. But JRY could not provide adequate employment due to corruption and leakages of fund and thus, failed to percolate benefits to the real poor. There fore, the scheme was restructured and streamlined with the introduction of a programme Jawahar Gram Samridhi Yojana (JGSY) (1999). The primary objective of JGSY was creation of demand driven community village infrastructure at the village level to enable the rural poor to increase the opportunity for sustained employment. With in the target group special safeguards have been provided to vulnerable sections by way of reserving 50% benifits for SC/ST 40% for women and disabled persons.

Prior to that in 1993, the Employment Assurance Scheme (EAS) was embarked upon. The primary objective of EAS is to provide gainful employment to the deprived groups for 100days of during lean agricultural season in manual work to all able-bodied adults in rural areas, who are in need and desirous of work, but unable to find it.

The secondary objective is creation of economic infrastructure and community assets for sustained Employment and development. Employment Assurance scheme is open to all rural people below poverty line. Preference is given to members of Scheduled Castes, Scheduled Tribe and freed bonded labourers: and at least 30% of Employment opportunities are to be reserved for women. While side works under the programmes (other than EAS) could be taken up during any part of the year, they should preferably be started during the lean agricultural season.

A salient feature of JRY was that it's financing as well as planning and implementation functions were devolved to the elected village panchayats. That scheme was expected to ensure better utilization of foods. In addition, the cost of administering the program was expected to decline.

The employment guarantee act, if effectively implemented would raise the purchasing power of the rural poor. This would lower the burden of food subsidies.

It needs to be noted that the implementation of employment

generation programme in the part has suffered from many flaws including the high incidence of leakages. As there are many irregularities it has been suggested that the only meaningful employment guarantee scheme would be one, which is not targeted, but is universal and demand driven.

What the rural poor need is not merely a guarantee of 100 days of work in year but uninterrupted employment for most part of the year.

Implementation is to be decentralized; control vested in local communities and gram sabhas. Transparency and accountability are to be ensured through in -built mechanisms for monitoring and social audit.

The work projects should be entrusted to the panchayats. Studies show that panchayats control increases participation, transparency and accountability.

The minimum wage under the Minimum Wages Act should be the floor wage. To talk of wages less than minimum wages is irresponsible and wrong. Such a wage fixation is will affect other provisions of the Act.

Also, when the household consists of several families the provisions of the Act are of no use. Hence, a household must be defied as a nuclear family.

The precautions that should be taken in the implementation of the Act have been well summed up (Patnaik, Prabhat, 2004, P.37):

"The scheme should be universally operated within a specified time horizon; it should be fully funded by the center; it should avoid tokenism (such as very low wages in the name of enlarging the number of beneficiaries) or targeting, and it should not occasion conflicts with other workers, employees or peasants."

Swarnjayanti Gram Swarozgar Yojana (SGSY) as the major on- going Programme for self-employment to remove poverty in rural areas has been implemented since 1.4.1999 merging the earlier schemes of TYRYSEM, DWCRA, MWS etc. for wage employment in the rural areas to take care of food security, additional wage employment and for laying village infrastructure at the same time.

The basic objective of the SGSY is to bring the assisted poor families above the poverty line by providing them income-generating assets through a mix of bank credit and Government subsidy. The programme aims at establishing a large number of micro- enterprises in rural areas based on the ability of the poor and potential of the area concerned. As a holistic programme of self- employment it covers all aspects of self- employment of the rural poor through the organization of Self Help Groups (SHGs) and their capacity building, training, selection of key activities, infrastructure development and marketing support.

A new wage employment programme namely the Sampoorna Grameen Rozgar Yojana (SGRY) has been announced in 2001.

Table 5.1 reveals the financial out lays under the SGRY increased significantly from 35.31 percent to 47.71 percent during 201-02 to 2003-04. The SGRY exhibited an increase from 5.43 percent to 7.79percent and rural housing from 16.59 percent to 18.50 percent during the said period.

Table 5.1
Financial Outlays of Central Government Schemes for Rural Development in India 2001-2004 (Rs. Crore)

Scheme	2001-2002	2002-2003	2003-2004
SGRY	3250(35.31)	4440(43.23)	4900(47.71)
PMGSY	2500(27.16)	2500(24.34)	2325(22.64)
Rural Housing	1527(16.59)	1725(16.80)	1900(18.50)
SGSY	500(5.43)	710(6.91)	800(7.79)
Others	500(5.43)	895(8.71)	345(3.36)
Total	9205(100)	10270(100)	10270(100)

Note: Figures in parentheses indicate the percentage to the total.

Source: Annual Reports 2001-02 and 2002-2003, Ministry of Rural Development, Government of India, New Delhi.

Macro analysis of Unemployment

During the period 1972-2000, employment grew at 1.97 percent per annum, while labour force grew at 2.01 percent per annum. As per NSS data, there were

3.98 million Unemployed in 1973-74 and their number have increased to 7.49 million by 1993-94 and as much as 9.15 million by 1999-2000 (Table 5.2).

Table 5.2

Number Unemployed and Incidence of Unemployment in Rural Areas 1973-74 to 1999-2000

	1973-74	1974-78	1983-84	1987-88	1993-94	1999-2000
Number of Unemployed (in millions)	3.98	7.14	5.95	9.14	7.49	9.15
Incidence of Unemployment (in %)	1.64	2.58	1.93	2.74	1.96	2.25

Source: NSSO surveys on Employment and unemployment.

Thus, while both growth in labour force and employment registered a decline in the last 20 years and also in aggregate terms (and especially between 1993-94 and 1999-2000), the decline in the growth of employment outstripped decline in the growth of the labour force (Desai and Das, 2004, pp.3045-51).

It is found that the growth rate of employment for the period 1987-88 was 2.03, which further declined to 0.58 percent in 1993-94 as per NSSO data. Also, it has been observed that at the All India level, number of unemployed on current daily status basis has increased from 19.5 million during 1993-94 to 26.44 million in 1999-2000 (Table 5.3). The planning commission has estimated that unemployment rate for the economy as a whole has increased from 8.87 to 9.11 percent in 2004-05.

Table 5.3
State-wise Number and Growth of Unemployed in India (DCS Basis)

States	Number of unemployment (CDS) (in million)	
	1993-94	1999-00
Andhra Pradesh	2.13(3)	2.66(4)
Assam	0.60(12)	0.67(12)
Bihar	1.86(4)	2.38(5)
Gujarat	0.98(8)	0.90(11)
Haryana	0.37(13)	0.29(15)
Karnataka	0.97(9)	0.98(9)
Kerela	1.64(7)	2.36(6)
Madhya Pradesh	0.94(10)	1.34(8)
Maharashtra	1.72(5)	2.68(3)
Orissa	0.88(11)	0.95(10)
Punjab	0.23(15)	0.34(14)
Rajasthan	0.26(14)	0.65(13)
Tamilnadu	2.91(1)	3.09(2)
Uttar Pradesh	1.64(6)	2.13(7)
West Bengal	2.46(2)	3.99(1)
All. India*	19.58	25.41
All India**	20.24	26.44

Notes: *Implies all India consisting of 15 major states only;
**Implies all India considering all states and territories.
Figures in parenthesis are ranks among 15 major states.

The annual growth rate of unemployment during the period 1993-94 to 1999-200 has been estimated as 4.5 percent. The vast majority of unemployed have been from rural areas in India. The share of rural unemployed was 73 percent during 1999-2000 in India. States like Bihar, Orissa, Andhra Pradesh, Assam, West Bengal, Kerela, Rajasthan, Haryana, Gujarat and Tamilnadu are reported to have more than 70 percent of rural unemployment in India (Bhaumik, S.K, 2003).

Employment and its growth in India

Employment and its growth in various sectors have been exhibited in table 5.4.

It is revealed from the table that next to agriculture, though manufacturing sector provides substantial employment has not indicated desired growth. Along with other Sectors manufacturing sector should be accorded priority as a vital source of employment.

It is revealed from the table 4.4 that there has been a decline in self-employment and an increase in casual employment during the period 1993-2000

Table 5. 4

Employment and Growth by the Sectors

Industry	Employed workers (million)		
	1983	1993-94	1999-00
Agriculture	207.23	242.46	237.56
Mining & quarrying	1.76	2.70	2.27
Manufacturing	34.03	42.50	48.01
Electricity	0.85	1.35	1.28
Construction	6.78	11.68	17.62
Trade	19.22	27.78	37.32
Transport, storage &	7.39	10.33	14.69
Common Financial services	1.70	3.52	5.05
Community, social & personal services	23.80	32.13	33.20
Total Employment	302.76	374.45	397.00

Source: NSSO surveys on Employment and unemployment

The proportion of regular salaried employment has remained more or less unchanged. An increasing trend of casuals employment has been depicted during the period under review. This phenomenon of increasing casual employment is because of non-availability of regular employment as well as their incapability of being absorbed in self-employment. Further, with the abundant supply of labour and extremely limited scope of organized sector employment, the employers will be in a position to employ at a lower wages.

The macro data clearly demonstrates that the unskilled labour absorption in future is more likely to take place in this sector in the absence of increase in organized sector employment. The usual status unemployment among the rural youth with secondary education and above was estimated at 12.5% (Radhakrishna, 2002).

There is wide spread concern that the acceleration in GDP growth in the post reforms period has not accompanied by a commensurate expansion in employment. Because of withdrawals from the public sector, there will be slow expansion of employment leading to a rise in unemployment rates.

Besides, relevance of unemployment among educated females in rural areas is about three times more than that of their male counterparts, presumably due to limited chances being open to them for migration to urban areas for securing employment.

Though women are increasingly employed in the post-reform period but they are by and large employed in low skill jobs, usually non-unionized, and experience adverse working conditions like low wages and long working hours (Dev, Mohendra 2000).

The characteristics features of the structure of the female work force in the nineties are an increasing feminization of the urban work force on account of an increased WPR for urban women, a declining share for women in rural non-farm employment largely in community and other services (Kalpagam, 2001).

Unemployment in Agriculture in Rural India

In rural India the deplorable fact is that due to the inadequacy of employment opportunities, scarcity of land, over dependence on agriculture, dependent on the gambling of monsoon; resulting in disguised unemployment declines in agricultural productivity.

Thus, agriculture in India provides seasonal employment to our population and as a result, the agricultural workers compete in the labour market in the informal services sectors.

As a matter of fact the marginal product of labour determines their wages, but marginal product of labour depends largely on the efficiency of the technology and on the land- to- labour ratio. Any change that would move labour from agriculture to other sectors would increase the land- to- labour ratio in agriculture and thus, ameliorate their economic conditions. Appropriate technologies with their enormous potentialities in enhancing the productivity of agriculture-based enterprises would help in creating employment opportunities. But over the years there has been decline in village industries on the wake of globalization and strong competitions at global level has made it a great problem for their survival and continuation.

A comparative analysis of NSS employment- unemployment surveys for 1993-94 and 1999-2000 reveals that between these periods, there has been a significant decline in the crude worker population ratio resulting in a slower growth of workforce relative to the growth in population and an absolute reduction in the number of women workers in rural India.

In terms of labour productivity, except for the construction sector, the gross value added per worker has grown significantly with a 6% per annum growth in the economy as a whole. This significant growth in labour Productivity has translated into an equally significant and wide spread growth in daily average wage earnings of casual wage labourers in rural India. In turn, this growth in real wage earnings has been significant to more than offset a reduction in the crude worker -population ratio to raise average wage earnings per capita at over 2.5% per annum in rural India during the period 1993-94 to 1999-2000.

Given the predominance of the agricultural Sector in the national economy in terms of employment, a meaningful employment strategy for rural India should accord high priority to the development of agriculture and allied rural sectors. Over the past three decades, the employment scene in India has undergone some significant transformations:

Firstly, although agriculture continues to occupy an important position in the Indian economy, its share in GDP has declined from 44.8% in 1977-78 to only 27.6% in 1999-2000 at constant 1993-94 prices. However, there has been very little decline in agriculture's share in employment: the share of employment in agriculture (UPSS) declined from 73.9% in 1972-73 to 60.2% by 1999-00 (Table 5.5).

Table 5.5
Share of Agriculture in GDP and Employment

Year	% Share of agriculture in GDP at 1993-94 prices	% Share of agriculture in employment (UPSS)
1972-73	44.8	73.9
1993-94	33.5	63.9
1999-2000	27.6	60.2

Sources: National Accounts Statistics and survey on employment and unemployment-various rounds.

Secondly, deceleration in the growth of employment during post-liberalization period from 1993-94 to 1999-00 has not been uniform across sectors of the economy. An important development that has been manifested is the sharp decline in employment growth in agriculture during 1990s (Table 5.6).

There are several reasons for the near brink of employment growth during 1990s in agriculture. One of the important factors was a sharp deceleration in the growth rate of agriculture in general and crop production in particular. The second reason for the decline of employment in agriculture is increasing capitalization.

On the contrary, in rural area, the non-agricultural sector has recorded a higher growth rate in employment than agriculture. Growth rate of employment in the non-agricultural sector was appreciably higher than that in agriculture over the period from 1972-73 to 1999-00. As a result, manufacturing, trade, transport and other service sectors have been emerging as important sources of rural employment.

Rapid agricultural growth generally triggers a higher growth in output and employment in non-farm sectors. In India, the emergence of numerous growth poles, including corridors of development along highways, and above all, public expenditure on anti-poverty and other rural development programmes and on rural infrastructure have been playing instrumental role in increasing output and employment in non-farm sectors.

Table 5.6
Growth Rates of Population, Workers (Employment) & Labour Force in Rural India

Population	2000-1994	1994-83	2000-83	2000-78	2000-73
	1.956	2.103	2.049	2.077	2.088
Workers (employment)					
a) UPS	1.557	2.105	1.905	1.919	Na
b) UPSS	1.030	2.037	1.670	1.789	1.936
No. of unemployed					
a) UPS	1.363	2.095	1.828	-0.247	Na
b) UPSS	1.482	3.316	2.645	1.138	3.136
Labour force					
a) UPS	1.551	2.105	1.903	1.842	Na
b) UPSS	1.040	2.063	1.690	1.774	1.960

Source: NSSO surveys for 1972-73, 1977-78, 1978, 1987-88, 1993-94 and 1999-2000. Na: Not available

This positive achievement in terms of rising productivity in agriculture and the process of diversification away from agriculture have been slow and halting. As has been evident from the table no 4.7, that from 1972-73 to 1999-2000, the share of agricultural labourers in the total labour force has declined only marginally from 73.9% to 60.2 %.

However, agricultural growth ought to act as an important engine of growth for other sectors of the economy, especially in rural areas. Thus, for rural employment a policy packages should be aimed at:

a) Accelerating the rates of sectoral and national economic growth,

b) Reversing the trend of deceleration of agricultural growth and public investment in agriculture,

c) Promotional policies for labour intensive and higher income generating allied agriculture and non-agricultural activities in rural areas for domestic markets, and

d) Diversification of agriculture towards hitherto neglected dry land areas in central and eastern regions are highly imperatives in order to boosting up agricultural production and rural employment and finally, assaulting on rural poverty.

Table 5.7
Employment Scenario in Indian States (CDS Basis)

Sl. No.	Selected States	Employment (,000) 1999-90	Employment Growth 1993-94 to 1999-00 (% P.A)	Unemployment Rate		GDP (% per annum 1993-94 to 1999-00
				1999-00	1993-94%	
1	Andhra Pradesh	30614	0.35	8.03	6.69	5.2
2	Assam	7647	1.99	8.03	8.03	2.7
3	Bihar	30555	1.59	7.32	6.34	4.5
4	Gujarat	18545	2.31	4.55	5.70	7.3
5	Haryana	5982	2.43	4.77	6.51	5.8
6	Himachal Pradesh	2371	0.37	2.96	1.80	7.1
7	Karnataka	20333	1.43	4.57	4.94	7.6
8	Kerela	8902	0.07	20.97	15.51	5.5
9	Madhya Pradesh	28725	1.28	4.45	3.56	4.7
10	Maha-rashtra	34979	1.25	7.16	5.09	5.8
11	Orissa	11928	1.05	7.34	7.30	4.0
12	Punjab	8013	1.96	4.03	3.10	4.6
13	Rajasthan	19930	0.73	3.13	1.31	7.0
14	Tamil Nadu	23143	0.37	11.78	11.41	7.1
15	Uttar Pradesh	49387	1.02	4.08	3.45	5.5
16	West Bengal	22656	0.41	14.99	10.06	7.3
17	All India	336736	1.07	7.32	5.99	6.7

Source: Planning Commission

It goes without saying that increased concern for human rights has provided a momentum for increased access to information right to work and abuses for denial of rights. If human welfare is the ultimate goal of development, providing basic human needs for all and guarantying decent work for the poor laborers must be the fundamental objectives. There should be rethinking about right in the context of work. The realization of rights in a broader economic, social and political context of development has emerged (Nayyar, 2003, pp.11-12).

To sum up, employment is the fundamental human right, which provides income to the labourers for their livelihood and sustenance. Devoid of employment the labourer is deprived of his purchasing power and therefore, his survival is endangered. Hence, employment is crucial and hence, the basic need for his livelihood. Therefore, the state must make adequate provisions for ensuring employment to the rural poor and unorganized labourers.

Effective monitoring of the Employment programmes is considered very important, particularly in view of the substantial step up in the allocation of funds for rural development programmes in the eighth and ninth five-year plans. It is well-recognized that the success of the programmes largely depends on the effective delivery system and efficient implementation at the grass roots levels so that the desired results could be achieved (Annual Report 2001-02 of Ministry of Rural Development).

REFERENCES

1. Annual Report 2001-02 of Ministry of Rural Development, Government of India, New Delhi.
2. Bhaumik, S.K (2003), Unemployment in India in the post liberation era, The *Journal of Labour Economics*, Vol. 46, No.1, p.726
3. Desai, Sonalde and Das, Maitreyi Bordie (2004) Is employment driving India's growth surge? A reality check, *Economic and Political Weekly*, vol.27, July 3-9, pp.3045-515
4. Kalpagam, U. (2001), Globalisation, Liberalisation and Women workers in the Informal Sector, in Amitabh Kundu and Alakh N. Shrma (ed.), *Informal Women Labour In India*, Institute For Human Development, New Delhi.
5. Mohendra Dev, S (2000), Economic liberalization and employment in South Asia-I & II, *Economic and Political Weekly*, vol. 35, Nos. 1, 2 & 3 January 8- 15, pp.40-51 and pp.135-147

6. Prabhat Patnaik (2004), Foundation Day Seminar on Guaranteed Employment for Rural Poor (November, 4-5, 2004), National Institute of Rural Development, Hyderabad

7. Nayyar, Deepak (2003), Work livelihoods and Rights, *The Journal of Labour Economics*, Vol. 46, January-March, pp. 11-12.

8. Radhakrishna, R. (2002), Agricultural growth, Employment and Poverty: A policy perspective, *The Journal of Labour Economics*, Vol. 45, No. 1, p. 9.

6

Tribal Economy: A Regional Study

(*A Study in Kondhmal District of Orissa*)*

Next to Madhya Pradesh, the state of Orissa has the largest concentration of tribal population in India. There are 62 tribes in Orissa with a population of 6.99 lakhs (1991 census) which constitute about 22.2 per cent of the total population of the state.

Tribals of Orissa

The Tribal population of Orissa are concentrated in almost all the districts of the state. As per 1991 census the largest concentration of such people is in the district of Mayurbanj where the tribal population is 57.8 per cent of the total population. The next in order of importance is the district of Koraput where the corresponding percentage is 54.3. The third place in this regard is occupied by Sudargarh with 50.7 percent of tribal population. Keonjhar with 44.5 per cent of such people and Phulbani with 37.3 per cent of tribal population occupies fourth and fifth place respectively among the districts of Orissa. The tribes of Orissa have distinct features.

As has been noted earlier the British Government followed a policy of exclusion or isolation towards the tribals. This was so because the administration of tribal areas was difficult and unrewarding. Besides, the British Government wanted to quaran-

*This is the revised version of the article appeared in S.N. Tripathy (ed.) *Tribals in Transition.*

tine the tribal people from possible political infection. Such a policy of exclusion might have been followed because of their conviction that the tribal people would remain happier and better if they were allowed to live as they were. This policy of isolation by the britishers insulated the tribal people from the main currents of the Indian life, and helped then to preserve their customs and tradition. But at the same time this hindered the growth of competence in them to face growing completion in a wider society to meet some of the challenges of the contemporary world.

After the Independence and even before the independence, the Christian missionaries and the Hindu Social reformers followed a policy of assimilation or detribalisation in an attempt to integrate the tribals with the national mainstream.

In view of the dangers of the above two extreme policies, after the independence attempts are being made to integrate the tribals with the national mainstream preserving their basic traditions, customs, culture and way of life. Here we notice 'duality' in the tribal development policy. There are elements of conflicts noticed in the formulation of tribal development policy by our planners and administrators. On the one hand, it is proposed to bring about progressive material advancement in such a way that they can be eventually integrated with the rest of the Indian people. On the other hand, it is emphasised to preserve and foster "all that is good and beautiful in their culture" and to do least violence to "the essential harmony of their lives". 'Tribal economy and culture' is, by and large, stagnant. It does not encourage and foster change. A major break with the tradition is a precondition to economic progress which is bound to necessitate drastic change "in the totality of social, cultural and religious institutions and habits and thus in their psychological attitude, their philosophy and way of life". Tension, again, is a price of progress. It is clear that if attempts are made to preserve the tribal culture uncritically, that will be fatal to their material welfare. In a dynamic world of rapid changes when different cultures are coalescing, it is pointless to advocate for preserving a definite culture. Planning implies priorities. 'Economic development' is the first consideration. Let the culture be planned to change its course compatible with development. Certain habits of the tribal people are inimical to progress, such as overemphasis on enjoyment and merry making, ritual and festivals that last for days together and their attitude of non-challenge towards future. Buffalo sacrifice* is still prevalent in Phulbani's Kondh community which look down upon the cattle. Cows are made to work in the fields thereby making them barren. Cattle is not reared with loss to agricultural production. This unhealthy tradition is inimical to development. The above tradition is one of the causes of protein-calorie deficiency and high infant mortality among the Kondh children. Moreover the retrogressive system of 'bride price' is antithetical to development. Adding fuel to the fire, the addiction to country liquor saps all energy, progressiveness, vitality from the tribals, young and old, men and women. These traditions, customs, habits, practices and way development of the tribal communities. The sectorial programmes in the sub-plan are different from the general programme, since the tribal genius, level of development, degree of sophistication, inclinations and aptitudes are different. Its resources are the sum total of resources of the State Plan for the sub-plan area, the central sectorial outlays, special central assistance and institutional finance. Emphasis has been given to core economic sector programme.

The objectives of the sub-plan are: (a) to narrow the gap between the levels of development of these areas and other areas; (b) to improve the quality of life of the tribal communities.

But these programmes, although laudable, could not achieve the proclaimed goal. Out of the States share of funds in the Fifth Plan, larger outlays have gone into infrastructural schemes and only 5 per cent of investment was for beneficiary oriented schemes. The poor performance was due to ineffective delivery system caused by inadequacies in the administrative machinery, lack of sensitive and trained management, lack of general preparedness for large investments, deficiency in accounting system, procedural delays and lack of proper monitoring and evaluation.

* Previously 'human sacrifice'

With the above discordant notes the Planning Commission formulated its policy for the Sixth Five Year Plan. It declared its intention "to wage an all out war on poverty" and "to create more equitable society". Emphasis was laid on comprehensive development plans instead of confining the programmes of mere educational incentives, grants and subsidies for economic activities, housing, drinking water, wells etc. The main thrust of the programme was four fold, namely: (1) integration of services at the delivery point to the beneficiary with a view to developing self-reliance in him, (2) development of services from the bottom upwards instead of top downwards (3) development of skills of diversify occupation, especially in the case of scheduled castes, and (iv) introduction of latest technology based on local materials and local sills to reduce drudgery of workers and also to remove the social stigma attached to their present profession.

The plans sought to generate and augment purchasing power through schemes like National Rural Employment Programme (NREP), the Integrated Rural Development Programme (IRDP). The Minimum Needs Programme was expected to meet the basic needs of the beneficiaries.

The system of tribal sub-plan was continued. The Sixth Plan realised the long time gap between the infrastructural development and its utilization by the beneficiaries. The Sixth Plan, therefore, reoriented its programmes in favour of family oriented schemes.

The emphasis was laid on the monitoring of the programmes. In view of the bitter experience about the lack of trained, sincere and committed administrative personnel, the Sixth Plan laid emphasis on supervision at the delivery points through an independent supervisory body constituted from among the members of the beneficiaries themselves. It also emphasized the necessity for imparting reorientation training of the officers operating at the different levels. A policy for a greater involvement of voluntary agencies was also enunciated.

The Seventh Plan continued to give a thrust to the occupational mobility and economic strength of the SC/STs. The strategy was designed to fulfil their minimum needs together with emphasis on the integration of different sectorial development programmes" at properly organising and modernising he artisans. The Plan proposed to have integrated and project based approach for development through ITDPs to create awareness among tribals against various types of exploitation. The planning process in tribal areas has to be a judicious mix of beneficiary oriented programmes, human resources development and infrastructure development"[3]. Concurrent evaluation and monitoring through the existing field functionaries in the tribal areas were suggested. The plan recognised the role of institutional finance in the beneficiary oriented programmes, public participation through decentraled planning, participation of voluntary organizations for implementing social economic programmes of the STs/SCs and generating right type of motivation in them.

Trend of Absolute Poverty in Orissa

As per our calculation based on the estimates of the Expert Group 1993, the absolute number of the rural poor in Orissa witnesses a rising trend during the period 1973-78, and 16.93 million in 1983-84. It is pertinent to state that, although the proportion of rural poverty has increased from 68.6 per cent in 1973-74 to 74.1 per cent in 1977-78 after which it has declined to 69.1 per cent in 1983-84, in absolute terms the number of the rural poor has increased during the said period. Beyond 1983-84, the number of the rural poor shows a marginal decline to 16.09 million in 1987-88.

Table 6.1
Absolute Number of Population below The Poverty Line in Orissa

Area	1973-74	1977-78	1983-84	1987-88
Rural	14.43	16.53	16.9316.09	
Urban	1.15	1.94	1.48	1.45
Combined	15.58	18.44	18.41	17.54

N.B. the figures are calculated on the basis of the estimates of the Expert Group 1993

In the year 1973-74 the urban poor is 1.15 million in Orissa. This number has risen to 1.94 million in 1977-78 after which there has been a steady fall upto 1.45 million in 1987-88. In the year 1973-74 the number of poor (both rural and urban at all Orissa level has been 75.58 million. It has risen to 18.44 million in 1977-78. Thereafter it shows a marginal decline in 1983-84. It further declines to 17.561 in 1987-88.

Magnitude of Poverty among the STs and SCs

As per the estimates of the Planning Commission, in 1983-84, 57.15 per cent of the ST population and 50.92 per cent of the SC population were below poverty line. In that year, the percentage of ST and SC population below poverty line in urban areas were 39.9 per cent and 40.4 per cent respectively in 1983-84.

A persual of the aforesaid analysis brings to light that in the state of Orissa, a high population of the people are below the poverty line. Especially in rural areas their percentage is high. The proportion of the urban poor is not less either too. Urban poverty is an offshoot of rural poverty since the rural poor migrate to the urban areas to seek employment and income.

The poor constitute mostly landless agricultural laborers and small landholders. The most of the poor people live in rural areas. The highest proportion of the poor are seen in hilly infertile areas with tribal concentration. The social and ethnic characteristics of the poor are exhibited with the downtrodden section of the society such as the scheduled castes. The ST and SC communities are mostly poor. Poverty is also associated with low level of aspiration. The poor are also lacking human capital. The quality of life among the poor is at a low level They have not gained access to social services like health and education. They have a low health profile and a low level of educational achievement.

Nearly 40 per cent of population of India are below the poverty line. The proportion of poor in Orissa is the highest in India (i.e. 60 per cent). Though the proportion of the poor has declined over a period of time the number of poor in absolute terms has increased. This increase is mainly because of growth of population in poor households. The condition of many poor must have stagnated over the decade.

Tribal Problems of Phulbani

The district of Boudh-Kondamals known as Phulbani, covers 7.11 per cent of the total area of the state and ranks sixth among the districts in size. Concentrate of tribal population is high in the district of Phulbani (39 per cent) as per 1981 census report. This figure is much higher than the state and national average of 22.43 per cent and 6.9 per cent respectively. The percentage of tribal populations falls by 3.8 per cent respectively. The percentage of tribal populations falls by 3.8 per cent from 1995 to 1981 as revealed from Table 6.1. The tribal females of the district outnumbered the males. Twenty-seven types of tribes are numerically important, found in Phulbani. They are Gond Khond or Kondha or Sita Kandha, Mirdhas munda, Pentic, Saora or Savor or Saura, Suabar or Lodha.[7] The tribals of Phulbani depend on agricultural holdings, which are small, scattered and uneconomic. The income from such uneconomic holdings is meagre. As a result, they remain below the poverty line. 'Podu' cultivation is practised in hill slopes mostly by the tribals who constitute 41 per cent of the total population of the district.[8] Due to lack of sufficient arable lands and ploughing equipment the Kondh tribes are habituated in Podu cultivation. This is considered as a laborious, dangerous and wasteful procedure of cultivation. The forest areas of the district are increasingly declining because of 'Podu' cultivation, large-scale deforestation. The total forest area of the district to the total geographical area was 82 per cent by 1975-76 and by 1980-81 it was reduced to 53 per cent.

The precarious condition of tribals in Phulbani are seen from their bad housing, education, asset position etc.

Living Condition of Tribals in Phulbani

The housing condition of the tribals is not good. Their houses consist of mud and wooden walls, thatched roofs and unhygienic surroundings. They conspicuously lack ventilation and lighting. Sanitation is absent. Cattle and men huddle is one room. There is no separate kitchen and therefore, Cooking is made in the same room where people live and take rest.

Condition of Health

The tribals, especially their children, suffer from malnutrition and related diseases. The growth of children gets stunted and they become easily susceptible to various diseases. Because of unhygienic living, lack of health consciousness, ignorance, and inadequate medical facilities, and, above all, owing to low economic status the tribals fall easy prey to killer diseases like malaria, meningitis etc. Sometimes, the epidemic of meningitis takes a heavy toll of lives in this inaccessible remote part of the country in the even of failure on the part of the authorities to take urgent and immediate remedial action. Malaria also causes havoc taking a sizable number of lives of the people. The sexually transmitted diseases like yaws and syphilis, skin diseases like scabies and anaemia etc. also occur. In the event of illness the tribals do not visit doctors they take recourse to sorcery of *guina* and village priests. The lack of health awareness accompanied by superstitions results in poor health of the tribals. Further, the habit of drinking saps all energy and vitality of the tribal people.

Status of Education

Most of the tribals are illiterate. They are superstitious as well. Their ignorance and lack of general awareness keep them underdeveloped through the ages.

Position of Infrastructure/Credit

Lack of infrastructure in the form of transport and communication, irrigation facilities, health services and marketing etc. makes the people impoverished and backward. The tribals face hardship during the period of scarcity of food grains in a year. During this part of the year the moneylenders-cum-traders take advantage of the situation. They lend money to the tribals and mortgage the produce of turmeric and other crops at a throw-away price. Thus the tribals do not obtain reasonable and fair price for their agricultural and forest produce. Sometimes the

Harijan moneylenders mortgage tribal lands taking advantage of the scarcity period and grab tribals lands in the event of nonpayment of the debt. Thus tribal land alienation takes place. It creates communal rift and dissensions which is one of the most important reasons of the recent communal killings among he Kondhs and Pans of the area. Because of excessive drinking habits some tribals fall prey to the evil designs of the moneylenders.

It is crystal clear from the illustration that poverty is rampant among the tribals of Phulbani with all its manifestations. To sum up, people suffer from poverty and unemployment, undernutrition, infant mortality, illiteracy, superstitions and ignorance. They are half-clad and they live in poor housing condition. They easily fall prey to empdemics and various killer diseases. Health services are quite inadequate. They lack health consciousness and hygiene. Their standard of living is low. Their diet mostly consists of rice and a pinch of salt only. Thus they lead a subhuman existence. The Kondh economy is thus primitive and backward, characterized by acute poverty.

During the post-independence era planned developmental efforts have been made to raise the economic condition of the tribal along with other rural people. To enhance their well-being specific tribal welfare schemes have been implemented. To safeguard their interest enforcement of protective enactments, constitutional provisions in the form of reservations have been undertaken. Through ITDAs and DRDAs several target-oriented antipoverty programmes are being implemented for generating employment and income. Infrastructural facilities in the form of roads, schools, dispensaries are also created. In spite of these efforts the tribals continue to be poorer. There has not been a perceptible change in their living conditions. They remain probably the most underdeveloped community in India.

Mortality is high for children in destitute families, but it is essential to ensure that some children survive to support the household in the parents old age, if not sooner. Even before they can earn income, children can free adults from various domestic tasks. Still many poor parents report that they want no more children and their last-born child had been unwanted. These couples often lack access to modern family planning services.

Poverty and hunger

Poverty and hunger among children is of particular concern. The very young are highly susceptible to disease, and malnutrition and poverty-related illnesses can cause permanent harm. Child poverty is strongly self-perpetuating. Child labour is common; many households depend on it, and much of the work has the social purpose of engaging the child in family activities. But work is often at the expense of schooling. For many poor people the opportunity costs of sending children to school outweigh the future benefits—especially for girls, whose economic value is often reckoned to be lower in various parts of the world. Some of the work that children do is highly exploitative; cases of debt bondage and of long hours worked in unhealthy conditions for low wages are widely documented.

Many of the poor have access to land without having ownership rights. Tenancy is common—although the poorest are often locked out of these arrangements because they lack the other resources needed for farming. Tenancy does not provide collateral or a secure hedge against risk and access to the land from one year to the next is often uncertain.

The poor are also lacking in human capital. Everywhere, they have a lower level of educational achievement than the population at large. Poor women often have too many children, spaced too close together, to the detriment of their health. The poor frequently suffer from hunger and malnutrition and from related illnesses. For instance, there had been high child mortality in Phulbani because of malnutrition for which the Government of Orissa had paid compensation to the tribal families where child loss had occurred. The susceptibility of the poor to malnutrition of hunger undermines their capacity for labour often their main or only asset.

The ownership of assets directly affects income opportunities without assets such as land, the poor must hire out their labour. Without adequate human capital they are limited to unskilled work. The elderly and physically handicapped may not even be able to offer their labour and may be forced to rely on charity. The importance of assets, broadly defined, suggests that policies should seek to increase the assets owned by the poor especially skills, health and other aspects of human capital and in agricultural economies, land.

The low proportion of irrigation, erratic distribution of rainfall, high periodicity of droughts and unfertile nature of the soil are the significant factors responsible for the backwardness of the district. Collection of minor forest produce is an important source of livelihood for the tribals.

A perusal of the study brings into light that decline in forest area due to 'Podu' or Shifting cultivation', restriction imposes by the government on the use of the forest by the tribals people, decline in the agricultural productivity, large-scale transfer of land to the non-tribals, uncertain rainfalls, frequent crop failures—all these entangle the tribals in the web of poverty and misery.

Government Policy

Protection of tribals from exploitation and their socioeconomic development have received attention of the government, after independence. Special safeguards were incorporated in the constitution of India and various problems of tribals came to the forefront. Article 46 of the constitution has clearly laid down that "the state shall promote the special case of the educational and economic interests os the weaker sections of the people and in particular of Scheduled castes and Scheduled Tribes, and shall protect them from social injustice and all forms of exploitation". Similarly, suitable provisions have also been made under the fifth and sixth Schedules of the constitution, particularly with preference from exploitation by moneylenders. The Orissa Transfer of Immovable Property (by Scheduled Tribes) Resolution, 1956 provides for the control and check of the transfer made by the Scheduled Tribes to the non-Scheduled Tribes in Scheduled areas. The Bonded Labour System (Abolition) Act, 1976 provides for the abolition of bonded labour system (Gothi) with a view to preventing the economic and physical exploitation of the weaker sections of the people.

Commendable efforts have been made during the plan periods for tribal development. One of the important problems of development in tribal areas is how best to reconcile the objectives of bringing about desired socioeconomic transformation and preserving their cultural autonomy. There has been increasing emphasis on ameliorating their economic condition, break the isolation of the tribal society and integrate them into the national mainstream.

Tribal Sub-Plan

Area having more than 50 per cent tribal concentration has been selected for the implementation of integrated Tribal Development Agency (ITDA) which serves as the unit of planning and executes development programmes. The tribals sub-plan aims at comprehensive development with focus on the individual family. The families living below the poverty line are identified, their needs and problems are reviewed, and appropriate programmes are executed. Apart from core economic sectors like agriculture, animal husbandry, horticulture, etc., sufficient emphasis was laid on education. In tribal areas infrastructure was poorly developed and therefore, capacity for the absorption of funds was very low. This problem is now mitigated by quantified investment in the tribal areas for infrastructure and individual family development.

There are two integrated Tribal Development Agencies functioning in Phulbani in the Sub-Plan area. Balliguda I.T.D.A. covers 9 blocks of Balliguda Sub-Division and Phulbani I.T.D.A. covers 3 blocks of Khondamals Sub-Division. The main thrust of I.T.D.P., as noted earlier, is two fold, i.e., development of initial infrastructure like communication, education, mini-irrigation and plantation and income generation of tribal families living below the poverty line.

A sum of Rs. 46.89 lakhs has been utilised by Balliguda I.T.D.A. and Rs. 95 lakhs by Phulbani I.T.D.A. in development of infrastructure. The amount has been spent on development of agriculture, in tribal welfare education institutions, supply of teaching aids to such schools, low cost hostels, plantation of minor forest produce, etc. The year wise expenditure during the sixth plan period is indicated in Table 6.2.

Table 6.2
Development of Information in Kondhmal District

Year	*Balliguda ITDA (Rs. in lakhs)*	*Phulbani ITDA (Rs. in lakhs)*
1980-81	7.45	3.95
1981-82	9.97	5.27
1982-83	3.65	5.86
1983-84	10.71	2.62
1984-85	15.11	6.25
Total	46.89	23.95

Source: District Rural Development Agency Office, Phulbani

In the state of Orissa there are 31.87 per cent of the total tribal population which are scattered in some areas and found in lesser concentration in other areas outside the Tribal sub-plan. Such tribal pockets are known as Modified Area Development Pocket (M.A.D.A.) for the dispersed tribals living in five Grampanchayats of Boudh Block of Phulbani District, M.A.D.A. Scheme is in operation since 1978.

Kutia Khond Development Agency (K.K.D.A.)

Kutia Khond is a primitive tribe living in the top of Belghar hill situated at a height at a height of more than, 2,000 feet above the sea level in Phulbani District. For their development a Micro Project, namely, 'Kutia Khond Development Agency' has been established in 1978.

Apart from the developmental schemes analysed above, some other development programmes like Drought-Prone area Programme (D.P.A.P.), District Rural Development Agency (D.R.D.A) and Fish Farmer's Development Agency (F.F.D.A.) are in vogue for alleviation of poverty and to bring about a change in socioeconomic life of the tribals. But so for, these agencies have not produced any visible transformation in socio-economic life of the tribals of Phulbani.

Despite developmental plans, spread of financial institutions, and other measures, it has been observed that the tribals are exploited by Mahajans and businessmen. The distressed sale of agricultural produce and forest collections by tribals to the Mahajans and businessmen have resulted in poor economic conditions of tribals.[9]

Therefore, it is highly imperative to develop the skill, knowledge and awareness among the tribal people coupled with income generating labour-intensive schemes i tribal areas through the development of agriculture, infrastructure, horticulture, etc.—which can bring about a catalystic change in their socioeconomic conditions.

REFERENCES

1. *Annual Administrative Reports of Scheduled Castes and Scheduled Tribes, 1960-61.* Tribal and Rural Welfare Department, Government of Orissa, pp.2-3.
2. Vidyarthi, L.P. and Rai, B.K., *The Tribal Culture of India*, 1977, pp. 412-14.
3. Tripathy, S.N. (Dr.) *Bonded Labour in India*, Discovery Publishing House, New Delhi (1989), p.80.
4. Bailey, F.G., *Caste and Economic Frontier (A Village in High Land of Orissa)*, Oxford University Press, 1962, p. 245.
5. Singh, S.K., *Tribal Society in India*, Manohar Publications, New Delhi, 1985, p. 18.
6. Nayak, R.K. (Dr.). Tribal World in Orissa in a state of Flux, *Social Welfare*, April 1990, p. 25.
7. Census of India, 1960, *Orissa District Census Handbook*, Boudh-Khondamals, pp. 15-16.
8. *Annual Administrative Report 1980-81 and 1981-82.* District Rural Development Agency (D.R.D.A.), Phulbani, p. 15.
9. Tripathy, S.N. *Bonded Labour in India, op. cit.*

7

Tribals in India: Problems and Policies

"Scheduled Tribes" (The word tribe is a controversial one. Various authors have opined that they are aboriginal, Adivasis, forest tribes, primitive classes etc. *Encyclopaedia Britannica* in its vol. 22, page 456 define s tribe as "a social groups of simple, kind, the members of which speak a common dialect, have a single government and act together for such common purposes as welfare".) are the indigenous inhabitants in India. They belong to different social stock, speak languages of different families and show considerable variation in their basic economy. Economically, they are the most vulnerable among the weaker sections of the community.

In India, according to the 1991 census the tribal population is 6.77 crores constituting 8.08 percent of the total population (Table 7.1). There are, in all 489 tribal communities including the sub-tribes, spreading all over the country. The tribal population is scattered all over the country except in the states like Haryana, Jammu and Kashmir, Punjab, Sikkim, Chandigarh, Delhi and Pondicherry. But in other states and Union Territories their concentration is quite high. Madhya Pradesh, Orissa, Bihar and Rajasthan alone accounts for nearly 60 percent of total tribal population in India.

*Also published in *Tribal Labour in India*.

The tribal communities are mostly concentrated in the following six regions.

Regions	States and U.T.
1. North-Eastern Region	Arunachal Pradesh, Assam, Manipur, Meghalaya, Mizoram, Nagaland and Tripura.
2. Himalayan Region	North Bengal, UP, HP.
3. Central India Region	Bihar, Orissa, MP. WB.
4. Western India Region	Gujarat, Maharashtra, Rajasthan, Goa, Dadar and Nagar Haveli.
5. Southern India Region	AP, Karnataka, Tamilnadu, Kerela.
6. Island Region	Andaman and Nicobar, Lakshadweep

Table 7. 1

Percentage of Scheduled Tribe Population to the Total Population of India

Census Year	Scheduled Tribe
1961	6.87
1971	6.94
1981	7.76
1991	8.08

Major Problems of Tribals in India

The tribal people are traditionally forest dwellers and they consider forests as their nourishing mother which supply them food, fuel and fodder. But with the shrinking forest resources their hardship increases. Not only that they are coiled with various other maladies relating to social, cultural, economic, demographic and infrastructural conditions. But this paper has sharper focus on some of the common economic problems of the tribals.

Agriculture

Agriculture is the main source of livelihood among the tribals in India. But due to poor soil, primitive method of cultivation and uneconomic holdings agriculture does not support them adequately. As a result, most of the tribals except few plain tribals are practising shifting cultivation as a method of agriculture from time immemorial. This type of cultivation is known by different regional names in India. It is called "Jhum" among the tribals of north-eastern region, "Bewa" or "Dahya" in MP and 'Podu" in Andhra Pradesh and Orissa. Shifting cultivation has been quite widespread in the tribal society as a way of life. But it is more prevalent among the 'Baigas' of Madhya Pradesh and 'Mundas' and 'Kondhas' of Orissa. In India about 9.3 lakh hectares of land are utilized for shifting cultivation.

Theoretically, shifting cultivation is now legally prohibited except in Bastar and Mandla of MP and North Eastern regions.

Shifting cultivation is not an ideal method of cultivation. It leads to soil erosion, and ecological degradation due to deforestation. This system of cultivation also promotes laziness and inertia among its practitioners. Notwithstanding its obvious disadvantages shifting cultivation cannot be stopped with one stroke as it has become a way of life of the tribals who have been practising it for generations. Unrewarding agricultural practices leads them to plunge in the quagmire of poverty and indebtedness and exploitation at the hands of non-tribals.

Indebtedness

Uneconomic land holding, growth of middlemen, unorganised money market, defective borrowing lending system and last but not least the extravagant habit of tribals on ceremonial occasions have thrown the tribals into the hands of unscrupulous money lenders. To the above fire other chronic problems such as illiteracy, ignorance and poverty worked as a fuel.

Indebtedness among the tribals does not have economic dimensions but social and psychological too. In many areas it leads to bondedness due to debt descending from generation to generation.

The system of borrowing in terms of kind is also vogue in many tribal regions. In Maharashtra this system is known by the name "Palemod" under which the tribal has to surrender a major portion or the whole of their crop to the moneylender during the time of harvest. Likewise in Tripura, a system of kind borrowing also prevails in Orissa called 'Gadi' in which the tribal has to repay the money lender double the amount borrowed by him prior to the harvest.

Indebtedness sometimes leads to loss of freedom and the consequent utilization of their labour power by the creditor and alienation of land and its acquisition by the creditor. The heavily indebted among them are incapable of breaking the vicious circle of indebtedness. The Koltas of Jaunsar Bawar (U.P.) are the classical example of the worst consequence of indebtedness.

Health

The tribals suffer from many chronic diseases but the most prevalent taking heavy toll of them are water-borne. This is mainly due to the very poor drinking water supply. Even when it is available in plenty, it is mostly dirty and contaminated. Diarrhoaea, dysentery, cholera, tape worms etc. are often the results of this situation.

Deficiency of certain minerals and other elements is also one of the reasons for diseases. In the Himalayan ranges there is "Goitre" a disease of the thyroid glands due to iodine deficiency. The incidence of venereal diseases is also very high among the tribals of certain parts of Himachal Pradesh, Uttar Pradesh, Madhya Pradesh, Andhra Pradesh, Bihar and Orissa. Tuberculosis is also common in many tribes.

In many interior areas tribals are reluctant to come forward for medical treatment because they have got their own system of diagnosis and cure. Medical personnel are contacted as a last resort.

Housing

Houses built for habitation in tribal India are of Kachcha and poor in construction and most of them are in the midst or on the outskirts of forests. A large number of tribal people are fortunate that they have been endowed with natural bounty. They are living in an ideal climatic condition free from any environmental hazard. Even some of the tribes of north-eastern region area experts in building beautiful houses with combining utility and artistic value. They are raised will off the ground and well ventilated and are kept spotlessly clean. Same is the case with other tribals like "Bagata" and "Koya" in A.P., "Gadaba" and "Saora" and Santhal of Orissa and Bihar. But all tribals are not fortunate in this respect.

A majority of tribals are homeless. Even they build their houses, these are below the satisfactory hygienic standards. Man lives along with domestic animals under the same roof making the living condition miserable.

Most of the houses provided by the government for needy tribals suffer from unimaginative and misfit designs. What generally happens is that some architect in the state capital who has never seen good tribal house or visited a tribe, draws up a type-plan which is followed automatically throughout the state. Any scheme of housing on stereotyped line without taking into consideration tribal customs, practices and superstitions are bound to meet the disapproval of the prospective inhabitants of the house.

Now-a-days Forest Department is another great hindrance in solving the housing problem of the tribals. The unimaginative and reckless bureaucracy has posed such reaction on the sue of forest wealth by the tribals that the entire forest policy has become counter productive in general, and to the housing in particular.

Education

The tribal people are educationally extremely backward which can be viewed from the census data. The census figures of 1931 disclosed that only 0.7% of the tribal people were illiterates. This percentage rose to 8.5%, 11.3%, and 16.11% in 1961, 1971 and 1981 respectively. The general literacy rate for these years stood at 24% (1961), 29.4% (1971) and 36.23% (1981). So the total picture of spread of education among the tribals is not very encouraging, barring a few tribes of north-eastern region like Khasi and Garo, who tremendously benefited from the vast network of Christian missionary institutions.

These are some reasons for which the tribal people are lagging far being their fellow country men. For example, more allocation of funds and opening of schools do not go far in providing education to the tribal people. It is a widespread feeling among he tribal that education makes their boys and girls defiant and insolent and alienates them from the rest of the society.

Some economic factors too are responsible for lack of interest shown by the tribal people in getting education. Abject poverty and subsistence living is responsible for most of the cases of dropouts. Sending a child to school tantamount to the same thing as loosing two healthy hands in the struggle for survival.

Most of the tribal languages and dialects are in the rudimentary stage and there is hardly any written literature. Hence, the problem of medium of instruction has been a great irritant.

Notwithstanding the above problems, the tribals suffer from a chain of sociocultural problems like alcoholism, drudgery, loose marital relations, superstitions and infrastructural problems like inadequate road, unsafe drinking water, lack of irrigation facilities etc. These problems keep them revolving round the vicious circle of poverty.

Tribal Development Policy

The Britishers followed the policy of isolation or segregation for the tribal mass due to the unrewarding nature of their economy and inaccessibility of tribal areas. The British Policy resulted in exploitation of the tribals by the money lenders, zamindars, contractors and non-tribals.

Constitutional Provision

The philosophy of tribal welfare policy is incorporated into the Constitution of India. It guarantees social equality, political justice to all irrespective of race and culture and offers equal opportunity of self-attainment. Under special provisions the tribal communities are to be integrated with the general social fabric of the country. Secondly, the socio-economic development of he tribes should be speeded up. Thirdly during the process of transformation their culture will not be deliberately multilated. Finally, all sorts of exploitative relationships with them shall be done away forthwith. The constitutional safeguards for the tribals are of protective, political and developmental nature. Article 15 of the Indian Constitution prohibits discrimination against the tribals. Provision of appointments, abolition of untouchability and forced labour respectively. Article 29 safeguards the interests of minorities in respect of their admission into the educational institutions. Protection from the social injustice, all forms of exploitation of STs is contemplated and provisions are made for the administrative control and welfare of scheduled areas and its people.

Table 7.2
Plan Period Strategies

S.No.	Plan Period	Tribal Developmental Programmes
1.	1st Five Year Plan (1951-56)	Community development Approach (Tribal Development Project)
2.	2nd Five Year Plan (1956-61)	Special Multipurpose projects for tribal people. (Creation of TD Blocks).
3.	3rd Five Year Plan (1961-66)	Improvement over the general CD approach (Improvement of TD Blocks)
4.	4th Five Year Plan (1969-74)	Administrative frame programme implementation and protective measures (Tribal Development Agencies (TDA)).
5.	5th Five Year Plan (1974-79)	Total and Comprehensive view of the tribal Problems and coordination of sectorial programmes (Tribal sub-plan and creation of Lamps)
6.	6th Five Year Plan (1980-85)	Integrated approach and large financial allocation (expansion of TSP).
7.	7th Five Year Plan (1985-90)	Mix-up of beneficiary oriented programme and infrastructural development (intensive Tribal Development)
8.	8th Five Year Plan (1992-97)	Plan Considering the need of the people and participation (District/Regional Planning and Participation of voluntary organisation)

First Five Year Plan

During the First Five year Plan Government of India had laid the foundation stone for the socialistic pattern of society based on democratic form without caste, class and privilege. The objective was to bring about the overall change of the tribes and tribal areas through Community Development Programmes (CDP). This policy favoured the tribals to adopt themselves into modernisation without sacrificing their own culture. Steps were also taken to meet the special needs of tribal people with respect to their culture, tradition and social psychological problems. Voluntary organisations were also encouraged to work in tribal areas. Most of the welfare measures were humanitarian in content and meant to health and educational benefits. During this plan the expenditure on tribals was 17.48 crores out of the total 2.25 crores our to the total population, the percentage expenditure on the development of tribals was only 0.83% of the total as against the tribal population which was 6.61 percent of the total population (Table 7.2).

Second Five Year Plan

During this plan a massive programme of integrated development was initiated through the National Extension Blocks (NEB) in tribal areas, each covering an average population of 25,000. A number of special blocks known as Special Multipurpose Tribal Development Block (SMPT) were introduced. This programme covered nearly 71% of tribal areas.

As per the recommendation of V. Elwin Committee SMPT Blocks were reorganised and renamed as Tribal Development Blocks (TDB). Each TDB was allowed to cover 25,000 tribals as against 65,000 in normal blocks and the geographical area of a block was kept at 150 sq. miles to 250 sq. miles. The Ministry of Home Affairs contributed Rs. 15 lakhs to each such blocks. The financial outlay of Tribal Development Blocks was considerably higher than the community Development Blocks. The total allocation of funds for tribal development was 0.87% of total plan outlay (Table 7.2.).

Tribal development policies were further reviewed by the study team on social welfare and welfare of backward classes.

The committee also warned against over administration in tribal areas by sending two officials and other to work among the tribal people.

Third Five Year Plan

In this plan various programmes were drawn up and were considered by he special working group in the light of the economic upliftment for rehabilitating the shifting cultivation. It recommended formation of multipurpose cooperatives for meetings the credit and not-credit needs of the tribal agriculturists and artisans. It laid emphasis on programmes like land improvement, land reclamation, social conservation, minor irrigation, supply of improved seeds and manure, bullocks, provision of training facilities and demonstration, fisheries, poultry, sheep breeding, organisation of training cum production centres and provision of assistance to village artisans. Education was given priority in tribal areas and stipends. Scholarships and freeships were also provided. In the medical and health care programme, the working group suggested preventive measure for diseases, provision of itinerant medical units for the treatment of ill and establishment of maternity and child welfare centres.

During this period a special committee was appointed by the Home Ministry. The committee recommended that the additional blocks in 3rd Plan period should not be confined to schedule areas but should cover other trial areas where their concentration is more than 55%. The working group recommended to open 480 blocks during this period. Integrated tribal development benefits were made available in tribal areas through 489 T.D. Blocks, on the basis of the recommendation of Elwin Committee and U.N. Dhebar Commission. Total expenditure on tribes during this plan was of the order of Rs. 52.55 crores out of a total of Rs. 8577 crores.

Fourth Five Year Plan

At the beginning of this plan P. Shilu AO committee reviewed the working of T.D. blocks in the country. It evaluated its success and made the following observations.

1. The performance of T.D. Blocks fell short of expectations.

2. Employment generation was narrow.
3. Schemes were tailored to suit the local people.
4. Developmental benefits were confined to the upper class tribal communities.

During this plan six pilot projects were introduced in the tribal areas covering about 40,000 tribal families with an investment of Rs. 1.50 crores per project. These projects were known as Tribal Development Agencies (TDA) and were taken up in the central sector. The Agencies adopt mostly agriculture veterinary services and fisheries as the core of economic sectors. The plan stipulated that 75% of the resources available under the head "Economic Development" for the T.D. and C.D. Blocks was to be earmarked for the schemes meant exclusively for the Tribals.

During this plan area approach programmes were started. Under this programme the T.D. Blocks were grouped into one or more Tribal Development Areas where special personnel were appointed at the District or sub-divisional level to look after the tribal needs. Local institution, specialists, nonofficial workers were allowed to take part in the preparation and execution of area development programmes. District level planning was given importance and experimental studies on growth centres for evolving strategy at the grass root level were taken up. The table depicts that the total outlay for the 4th Plan is approximately double that of the 3rd Plan, whereas the plan allocation for tribals is less than one and half times the 3rd Plan. Consequently the percentage share of Tribal expenditure has declined (Table 7.2).

Fifth Five Year Plan

Due to unsatisfactory and slow process of development tribal areas, varieties of schemes and programmes were launched during this plan. A new strategy was evolved for planning and development of the tribal areas through sub-plan approach. The sub-plan guidelines were issued by the planning Commission. The main objectives of the sub-plan were to eliminate all forms of exploitation, boosting up the process of socioeconomic changes, buildup an inner strength of the people and improve the organisational capabilities of the tribals.

The Planning Commission emphasized on the sociocultural development of tribal communities, nature of physio-geographical condition of the area, the pattern and practice pertaining to various productive activities, pattern of ownership of means of production and the legal framework, particularly in respect of land ownership, land tenure and transfer.

The new approach of the 5th Plan covered about 65% of the total tribal population of the country. Highest priority was given to elimination of exploitation of tribes as a first step for economic upliftment. Basing on the guidelines of the sub-plan approach, ISO ITDP's were introduced.

But it is observed that the sub-plan approach had limited success, due to the administrative inadequacies, lack of managerial skill and lack of proper monitoring, and evaluations. The benefits of the development schemes followed to the well-to-do sections of the tribals and non-tribals. Again, since most of the tribal areas are inaccessible with scattered habitations, gain from various schemes could not reach the tribals.

Sixth Five Year Plan

The basic objective of the 6th plan was to bring the entire tribal population under suitable development programmes. The gap between level of development in the tribal areas and the surrounding areas was to be bridged by the end of 6th plan. The broad approach to tribal development was not only to bring development to the tribal concentrated areas but also to revitalise the dispersed and primitive tribals.

The sub-plan approach was allowed to continue as a strategy for the concentrated areas. But for the dispersed tribal areas two important approaches were lunched viz. (i) Modified Area Development Approach (MADA) and (ii) Community Development Approach (CDA). For primitive tribes special income generating schemes were introduced during this plan.

The development approach of this plan can be divided into four major parts viz.

1. Integration of services at the delivery point to the beneficiary with view to self reliance in him.
2. Development of services from the bottom upwards in stead of top downwards.
3. Development of skills to diversify the occupation.
4. Introduction of modern technology based on local materials and local skills to remove social stigma attached to their present profession.

Further the plan proposed to reform garnets and subsidy system so that the beneficiary becomes self-reliant over and specified period.

Seventh Five Year Plan

During the 7th Five Year Plan a coordinated approach was proposed along with an appropriate administrative structure in tribal areas. Main attentions were given not only for he socio-economic development of tribal areas but also for the development of agriculture, horticulture, forestry and village and cottage industries which would make the tribals to cross the poverty line. Suitable steps were proposed to be taken to eradicate their exploitation in the fields of money lending, land transfer, debt bondage, forestry, trade and sociocultural spheres. States were directed to bring the tribal women and children into the direct fold of economic development. The LAMPS and TDCC were strengthened for the elimination of exploitation in the field of marketing of minor forest produce of the tribes. Appropriate guidelines were introduced in favour of the state during this plan to undertake the followings for the tribal areas. (a) cabinet subcommittee was formed to decide broad objectives of the tribal sub-plan (b) tribal representative were associated with plan implementation, (c) ITDP's should be given full control, (d) prohibition of transfer of tribal lands to non-tribals and (e) dedicated services of the officers.

An intermediary formula between agriculture and shifting cultivation was also though of for the tribal area to restore ecology. A policy for the rehabilitation of displaced tribals of development project areas were undertaken.

Eighth Five Year Plan

In order to intensify integrated efforts vigorous programmes and schemes were outlined for tribal areas for the removal of development bottlenecks, elimination of exploitation, oppression, suppression of money-lending businessmen, nonpayment of minimum wages and right to collection of minor forest produce (MFP) etc. during this plan.

A frontal attack on tribal poverty, illiteracy, ignorance and exploitation is made through special component plan, TSP and other special component plan, TSP and other special schemes. Cooperatives are designed to render services in tribal areas mainly for marketing of SAP and MFP.

Forests sustain major part of the livelihood of tribals. In order to develop a systematic relationship between tribals and forests, the government has formulated a forest policy. As per the provisions of this policy various schemes like watershed projects, sectorial programmes like agriculture, social forestry horticulture, infrastructure and social services have been introduced in order to divert the tribals from the practice of shifting cultivation. State governments have been advised to convert the forest villages into revenue village after proper notification to generate and explore forest resources.

It appears that elaborate care has been taken during different five year plans to spell out tribal development strategies for promotion, for welfare and socioeconomic upliftment.

Conclusion

Economic prosperity and social change imply radical transformation in the lives of tribals. The policy of isolating followed by the Britishers only preserved their cultural heritage. By and large, all the tribal policies followed during the plan periods are more welfare oriented rather than developmental in nature. Since the socioeconomic conditions of tribal groups in different regions differ considerably, no blanket scheme can be successful. Taking into account the differences specific schemes suitable to local conditions should be drawn up for the purpose of development.

REFERENCES

1. L.P. Vidyarthi, *Tribal Culture in India*, Concept Publishing Company, New Delhi - 1985
2. K.S. Singh, *Economics of the Tribes and their transformation* (ed.), Concept Publishing Company, New Delhi, 1982
3. Elwin Verrier, *New Deal for Tribal India*, Ministry of Home Affairs, Government of India, 1963, New Delhi.
4. B. Chowdhury, *Tribal Development in India* (ed.) Inter India Publication, Delhi 1982.
5. Census India, 1991 Registrar General, India.
6. D.R. Pratap, *Approach to Tribal Development* (ed.), B. Chowdhury.

8

Tribal Labour Out-Migration*

Mankind has witnessed migration since time immemorial. Wars persecution, climatic changes and economic forces have been the principal movers of people. In this paper an attempt has been made to focus on the genesis and consequences of labour out-migration in India with reference to Orissa.

Labour is the crucial factor of production. It turns other resources into goods and income and thus, to the satisfaction of the needs of the population. It is a fact that out-migration of labour which overwhelmingly occurs from the poorer regions of a country to the richer regions of other countries, helps the migrant receiving regions more than the migrant-sending regions in terms of production of goods, generation of income and the satisfaction of needs.

Genesis of Labour Out-migration

Ever since Columbus discovered India, he planned to supply slaves to the motherland in return for breeding cattle, seeds and foodstuffs from Spain. 'Indian slaves' he wrote, 'could provide cheaper labour for Europe and compensate for the financial expenditure required on overseas expeditions.' Indian slavery was the first large-scale system in the history of capitalism to exploit the workers of conquered territories outside Europe to any great extent.

*Also published in the, *Studies in History and Culture*, Vol. 6, No. 1 and 2, 1998.

Coolie Labour

The coolie system (coolieism) came into being during the second quarter of the 19th century, even before the abolition of slavery. Coolieism was a mixture of various labour systems and stood somewhere between slavery, forced labour and debt bondage on the one hand and free wage labour on the other. It contained elements of all these systems.

The very devices which caused underdevelopment in India, also had the effect of assigning to the subcontinent the role of supplier to the world market of both raw-materials and human labour power. Those devices included robbery, war and plunder, but also certain economic and custom policies, the break up of village communities, the dismantling of social structures and the neglect of public works. The development of the irrigation system was a prerequisite for agricultural production in many parts of Asia and also in India.

But the decay of the irrigation system reduced the agricultural output and simultaneously destroyed the handicrafts and nascent industries, all of which forced the population back on to the land. These processes of changes resulted in famine to take a hold in India since the end of the 18th century. Famines occurred in 1770, 1784, and 1837, in 1861 in Bengal and northern India, in 1877 and 1900 in other parts of India. In 1834 Lord Cornwall is claimed that 1/3rd of the regions of Hindustan that were controlled by the East Indian Company and that had one been densely populated were nothing more than jungles inhabited only by wild animals.

As the rulers of India, the British established sole control over the second largest supplier of coolie labour in the world, the first being China. They used this reservoir of labour first and foremost for their own colonies in the USA, Asia, Africa and Australia but from time-to-time they also permitted the recruitment of labourers by other colonial powers.

Magnitude of Coolie Migration

The statistics available on the subject of coolie migration are fragmentary and complex. Between 1854 and 1867, 3,66,000 Indian indentured labourers were exported to Mauritius. About

4,30,000 Indian labourers were imported into seven British colonies in the Caribbean including British Guina between 1838 and 1918. The majority were indentured labourers. The records show 60,965 Indian coolies were imported to work on the plantations of Fiji between 1879 and 1916.

India's export of coolies, which started in 1830's, had been preceded during the second half of the 18th century by the sale of Indians from the south of the country as slaves. It had been estimated that in 1921, there were 2.5 million Indians living abroad of which 2 million came originally from the Presidency of Madras.[2]

Thus, the emigration of Indian labour began with the abolition of slavery in the British Empire in 1834. It arose from the need of British planters in the tropical and the subcortical colonies for a regular supply of agricultural labour. The shortage of agricultural laborers emerging out of the virtual refusal of the Liberated slaves to work in the sugar plantations of Mauritius, British Guiana, Trinidad and Jamaica threatened the existence of sugar industries there. The labourers saved the colonies form impending disaster but for whom the estates would have been utterly ruined and abandoned.

In the thirties and forties of the last century, the recruiting ground was mainly the tribal regions. Most of the emigrants wee so called 'hill coolies' who were recruited from Chhotonagpur division, Shahabad, Bankura, Birbhumi and Burdhawan districts of Madras Presidency. The hill-coolies were considered suitable due to their experience of working in the jungle lands, their docile nature and simplicity. The recruiters on false promises could easily recruit them. But their number gradually decreased after 1840's because of the heavy mortality at sea among this class of emigrants and partly due to completion of the tea districts of Assam. Therefore the main recruiting operations were pushed westward into the Bihar and modern Utter Pradesh regions. In the south India, the main recruiting districts were Trichinopoly, Madurai, Tanjore, Coimbutore, Salam Nellore, Chingleput, Hyderabad, Rajmuddry, Bangalore, Vijianagaram and Madras.[3]

The oppression of the landlords and money lenders made

the poor hill people paupers and they became easy prey to the unscrupulous recruiters. Dalton says that they had a tradition of migration because of their object condition and therefore, they were easily induced to migrate to other parts of the country and even to foreign lands.[4]

Wage discrimination though undoubtedly significant, was not only form of sexist exploitation and oppression to which female Indian coolies were subjected. The fact that female labourers were in the minority gave rise to all kinds of sexism, and female coolies had to ensure for greater exploitation, misery and injustice than their male counterparts. In addition to working on the plantation, workers also had to take care of the children in particular and their men. This meant that women were responsible for household chores, but more important that they were exposed to the most extreme forms of sexual exploitation.

For women, then, collieism meant being raped by fellow labourers, by foremen and by plantation owners, from whom even marriage did not protect them to any extent. Although women were widely traded and prostitution was practices, the form of exploitation to which women were most commonly exposed under the coolie system must have been polyandry, into which women were forced in Mauritius and Fiji.

Coolieism, in which physical violence and punitive sanctions played important roles, significantly aided the establishment of structures which guaranteed an adequate system of labour power for measures other than economic pressures. In many territories, including those where in the past it had only been possible to recruit labour by force, migrant labour and labour migration now appeared to offer a prospect, an alternative to hunger and poverty. In the backdrop of the above analysis let us examine the problem of out-migration in the tribal districts of Orissa.

Labour Out-migration in Orissa

Migration either within the state or interstate, effect the distribution of resources-especially, human capital. The economic and social effects of migration are important to the development of both the places of origin and those of destination. The direction of flow from rural to urban area, affects the regional development of the place of migrants origin and contributes to the problem of urban growth.

The rural development of Orissa get a continuous set back due to labour out-migration as the state is deprived of its work force which if absorbed inside the state will uplift the economy from poverty and stagnation. The Royal Commission on Labour (1929-31) observed that Orissa labourers used to go Rangoon, Assam, Bengal and Bombay since 1803 in order to work in plantations, dams, roads, railways, jute mills, textile mills etc. To eke out a living, the labourers of Orissa migrate to distant parts of the country being forced by natural calamities like famine and high pressure of population on land, absence of alternative avenues of employment etc. The exploitation by the feudal lords in the princely states of Orissa had worked as a push factor for such out migration.[5]

A large segment of migrant labourers in Orissa belong to the category of landless agricultural labourers, and often to backward tribal communities. In few cases those who have limited land didn't possess the needed resource to develop the same and as a result, the barren land is left uncultivated for years. Therefore, they are, compelled to work as agricultural labourers in the land of the big landlords or zamindars of the same village or adjoining villages. The employment being seasonal and the wages being low, they find it hard to make both ends meet. Thus, the insufficiency of such labourers' income to cover up the living expenses even on a subsistence level seems to be the basic underlying factor of their indebtednes.[6]

Further, the social customs and obligations like births, marriages, death in the families and drinking habits play an important role in forcing the poor to resort to borrowings. The money lenders used to take advantages of the deteriorating economic conditions of the poor. They advance small loans from time to time in exchange of binding them to work as agricultural labourers till the final payment is made. Thus, indebtedness has been generally believed to have emerged as a factor challenging he economic self-sufficiency of such labourers who find it difficult to repay. Their dues accumulate very fast under exorbitantly high rate of interest. They find it impossible to extinguish there debts and begin to work for the creditor at extremely low wages and venture to repay the debt by their hard labour. At this critical time, the *Sardars* and *Khatadars* the recruiting agents of brick-kiln owners or stone quarry lessees or construction of project contractors, approach such labourers. They make false promises and allure the poverty stricken labourers to the distant lands.

As each labourer is paid a part of his due for the labour he would render before he goes to the work-site in advance and the rest after the period of contract is over the practice followed is well named after the *Dadan* labour. The agricultural labourers unable to understanding the problems and agony involved at the time of receiving such advance from the recurring agents or contractors.

Elements of Exploitation

The tragic fact is that no sooner they reach at the work site, than all the hopes disappear and promises make to them undermine. Moreover, they are subjected to a chain of merciless exploitation in the hands of *Munshis* of the brick-kiln owner or stone quarry lessees. They are made to work pretty ling hours, not being provided with medical benefits, proper food and shelter. Illiterate and ignorant of any other language except Oriya, they fail to put forth their legitimate grievances before the local non-Oriya authorities and therefore, the letters in all possible manner fail to come to the former's rescue. The *Dadan* labour of Orissa are taken to far off placed like Jammu and Kashmir, Meghalaya, Sikkim and even to the Arabian countries like Iraq and Iran. The recruitment of Dadan labourers in Orissa is made mostly from the rural and tribal areas of Keonjhar, Mayurbhanja, Sambalpur, Bolangir, Kalahandi, Ganjam and Puri districts.

Tribal Migrants of Orissa

In Bolangir, Kalahandi and Phulbani—the backward districts of Orissa, because of the deforestation, increased pressure on land, lack of irrigation and recurring drought conditions due to poverty and unemployment, tribals have been migrating to outside villages, districts and state for periods ranging form 2 to

6 months for working in construction projects, bricks-kilns and tea estates.

Exploitation of tribal and agricultural labourers is common phenomenon in Patnagarh and Titilagarh Subdivision of Bolangir. Earlier, it had been observed that the economic plight put them almost in the point of starvation leading to pledge the services to the *gantias*.

The Brick-kiln Migrant Labourers

It has been observed by the researchers that every year between March and June thousands of tribals from Bolangir and Kalahandi migrate outside the state in search of employment. They are employed in brick industries located at Patrapur, Itchapuram, Palasa, Srikakulam in the neighbouring state of Andhra Pradesh. They toil hard from 6 a.m. morning to 10 p.m. night. There is no specific work-hour and as a result, the more they work, the more they earn. For each piece of brick, they get 20 paise only. Each brick-kiln labourer builds at least 600 bricks each day, labouring for 12 to 13 hours. For preparation of clay, water and mixture for bricks they devote the morning hours and in the afternoon shifts they construct bricks. Such tribal labourers of Bolangir and Kalahandi are mostly unskilled. However, they are habituated with working in brick-kiln industries. They move in group along with their wives and children who also put hard labour for their survival. They could not understand Hindi nor could not speak Oriya language properly. Some of them are also found in various brick-kilns of Berhampur, Purusottampur, Sheragada in Ganjam district of Orissa.

It is revealed that factors like famines, loss of land through indebtedness, acute unemployment in the place of origin, caste disabilities, destruction of village crafts are push factors of the tribal migrants of Bolangir and Kalahandi.

Medical facilities, weekly holidays, statutory leaves, bonus and other labour laws are never observed in case of such tribal migrants of Bolangir and Kalahandi. They work in the filthy working conditions, devoid of safety measures. They suffer from tuberculosis, asthma, respiratory infections and lung-cancer but no medical assistance is available to them. The tribal migrants are docile, submissive and subservient to the employer. Some agricultural labourers from Bolangir and Kalahandi are also found migrating to Rajpur. Jagdalpur, Nagpur and Surat for working in various construction projects and to pull rickshaws.

The foregoing analysis reveals the fact that labours out-migration has been a continuous phenomenon in our country, and more correctly among the poor segments of the society. It should be kept in view that migration being the movement of human being sin pursuit of certain cherished objectives like better employment, better wages and better quality of life, there is apparently nothing wrong. However, the problem is of serious magnitude when such migration leads to human misery and exploitation. It is seen that attempts to stem the tide of labour migration in Orissa have not been successful. What does seem apparent is that unless the socioeconomic circumstances of the sending and receiving areas alter radically, the labour migration in Orissa will continue, spelling disaster and despair to the economy. The urgent need of the hour is heavy investment in the traditional sector as well as in industrially backward regions for adequate employment creation. Since modern manufacturing industries are expected to absorb only a limited number of labourers, adequate employment can be created in small-scale industries, construction works, labour-intensive road works afforestation, animal husbandry, fishery and the like.

REFERENCES

1. Lydia Potts. The World Labour Market (A History of Migration), Translated by Terry Bond, (Zed Books Ltd., London, 1990), 73.
2. *Ibid.*, 80
3. Panchanan Saha, *Emigration of Indian Labour* (1834-1900): (Peoples Publishing House Pvt. Ltd. New Delhi, 1970), 28-31.
4. *Ibid.*, 41-42.
5. *Report of the Royal Commission on Labour in India* (1983): Agricole Publishing Academy, (Reprinted, New Delhi), 14-15.
6. S.N. Tripathy, *Bonded Labour in India*, (Discovery Publishing House, New Delhi, 1989), 15.
7. Nilamani Senapati, (ed.). *Orissa District Gazetters* (1968) *Bolangir*, Chapter XVII, (Government Printing Press, Cuttack, 1968), 466.

9

Shifting Cultivation in Tribal Orissa*

Known by different names in tribal India, shifting cultivation is called as 'Jhum' in the North East, Kurao and Khullu in Bihar, Waler in Gujarat, Penda, bewar and duhiya in Madhya Pradesh, Kunri in Tamilnadu, Bringa, Podu, dahi and Koman in Orissa. The land use system is specially restricted within hill slopes below 1000 meters, where we notice high rainfall with low density of population. Depending upon physiography, rainfall, temperature, soil and density of population shifting cultivation as a suitable method of land use has been practised in tribal India for centuries. Thus, shifting cultivation is an age-old method of land use, a piece of land is selected, most of the trees and bushes are cut down and set on fire after exposing them to sun. On this land a variety of mixed crops is grown generally for two to four years. Subsequently, the shifting cultivators abandon the plot and search for another plot for such type of cultivation.

The important features of shifting cultivation are:

1. Rotation of fields;
2. Slash and burn operation;
3. Keeping land fallow for a number of years for regeneration of forests;

*Also published in the book, *Tribals in India: the Changing Scenario*..

4. Use of human labour as chief input;
5. Non-employment of drought animals; and
6. Use of simple implements such as dibble sticks, scrappers etc.

In India, shifting cultivating is carried out on a large scale in many tribal belts. It has been estimated by the Task Force on shifting cultivation set by the Ministry of Agriculture, Government of India, that approximately 9.95 million hectare land under shifting cultivation. About 225 development blocks in 62 district in 16 states are affected by this cultivation. Indeed, shifting cultivation is practised by 12 per cent of the tribal population in India.

The data available with regard to magnitude of shifting cultivation are unreliable and hence are not dependable.

The unreliability of the data can be testified if those relating to one state like Orissa are examined. E.U. Moonly in 1951 had reported that almost 100 per cent of Koraput was under shifting cultivation. The corresponding figure, as per the Forest Resource Survey conducted in 1971-72 by NCAER was 36.82 per cent.[2] But in 1983-84, the Government of Orissa reported 42.66 per cent of the area of Koraput as under shifting cultivation. Apparently, all these diverse figures reveal the undependable data pertaining to shifting cultivation. It has been observed that money-lenders from outside have appropriated tribal land and are using it for shifting cultivation, not for survival but for commercial purposes.

It has been further, pointed that shifting cultivation is being practised in 10 districts of Orissa. According to an estimate, the effected area under shifting cultivation is 1,84,018.46 hectares. Table-1 reveal the area under shifting cultivation. The data have been collected, by manual interpretation of land Sat-I imagery.

The primitive tribals, who are the main residents of these districts practise shifting cultivation extensively in the area, by cutting down the forest vegetation. Recent assessment of the area under active Podu (shifting cultivation) in these districts is shown in table 1.

Within the state of Orissa, shifting cultivation is known in different names. It is known as 'Dangar Chash' or hill cultivation in Kalahandi. In Redhakhole and Bunra, where shifting cultivation is practised in very limited areas, it is called 'rama' the Khondsi inhabiting the areas. The Bhuyans of Pallahara, Bonai and Kenonjhar call it 'biringa'. In the southern parts of Orissa, Podu cultivation is also known as 'gudia' or 'jhuming'. 'Dahi' or 'Dahia' is the term used in the western parts of Sambalpur, but is less pernicious as an agricultural practice in that branches of trees cut are spread over settled cultivated fields and burns so as to have a stimulating effect of the ashes on the crop. The other type of 'dahia' is that a forest growth on a neighbouring hill-slope is burnt before monsoon sets in so that the first sowers wash down the ashes into the cultivated fields on the foot of the slope to enrich production. This practice is very popular is Sambalpur district and particularly in the Nawapara subdivision of Kalahandi.

Table - 1

Area Under Shifting Cultivation as Assessed from E.R.T.S.

Sl. No.	Name of the District (Undivided)	Area in Hect.
1.	Bolangir	1,795.40
2.	Dhenkanal	5,121.20
3.	Ganjan	21,680.30
4.	Kalahandi	5,861.40
5.	Keonjhar	40,638.16
6.	Mayurbhanj	7,303.40
7.	Koraput	30,651.16
8.	Phulbani	20,995.66
9.	Sambalpur	41,781.00
10.	Sundargarh	8,190.74

In the areas, popularly known as the Ganjam Malayas and

in the District of Koraput, shifting cultivation exists in the most extensive and destructive manner. The occupation of the hill people is mainly agriculture and collection of forest produce. In certain cases, shifting cultivation is generally subsidiary occupation for the hill-royats while in certain remote parts Podu is the only means of subsistence. The hill tribes that take recourse to it in Ganjam Malayan are the Khonds in Balliguda and Phulbani regions where as it is practised by the 'Souras' in Parlakhemundi in R. Udayagiri Taluks of Gajapati District. The tribal people who resort to shifting cultivation in Koiraput (undivided) are Khonds, the Koyas, the Souras, the Gadabas, the Parjas and Bonds.

The genesis of shifting cultivation is manifested among the primitive tribes, has a historical background. Most of the people of the Agency areas were tribals like Khonds and Savars. Both hill officials known as muthheads and the people of the plains also exploited their in numerous ways. This was the primary cause of the rapid impoverishment of the tribal peasantry. The extreme poverty compelled many tribals to sell or mortgage their lands to the people of the plains. A result of which, the tribals of the region were driven to inaccessible forests and hilly areas where they maintained their simple life style and survival-oriented culture. The agents of the 'new order' represented by traders, money lenders and contractors did not leave them there either. The outcome of this oppressive 'new order' was that the 'tribal poor' have found themselves exceedingly indebted and alienated from most of their land except for a few pieces of eroded land strips.[4] Thus, the tribals form time-time-time; were deprived of their moire fertile lands and were subjected to ruthless exploitation by the invading people which has resulted in the hill-men's flying in greater and greater wilderness. The infiltration of the people from the plain continues resulting in depriving the hill-men of all good lands they reclaimed. When deprived of all settled cultivation a hill-man is left with very little choice for his existence and shifting cultivation for him is the easiest means for his survival. Being constrained to live in wild conditions and without the opportunities of a modern life a hill-man has to develop a life in accord with the natural surroundings in which he lives and hence, develops a very superstitious mode of living and thus, shifting cultivation forms often religion-cultural part of his existence.

Apart from this, when migration of the hill-man into the forest began in primitive days and continued for years, there was no authority to intervene and there being rival for a hill-man his original selections for 'Podu' were the plainer lands but in course of time, opium vendors and 'Sourcars' who came from plains immediately acquired ascendancy over the hill-man's possessions who in despair migrated into the inaccessible tracts and cultivated the hill-slopes. It has been observed that if a suitable land was once found in possession of an Adivasi it was not to remain in his possession for any length of time because of the covetous eyes of Sowcars, Sundhis, Panos and such of the like. Consequently, by long standing practice the hill-tribes abandon old villages and form new ones. This habit is at once the cause and effect of shifting cultivation.

Thus, shifting cultivation seems to be the natural consequence of centuries of struggle both warlike and economy for the Adivasi who has lost the ground everywhere. Moreover, because of the aborigines', lack of resourcefulness, inferior complex and primitive conservatism, his shifting cultivation is not supplemented by any other avocation so as to supplement it ultimately. With the growth of population, the demand for cultivable land increased and as a result, the tribals have to search out new hill slopes for their purposes.

The economic reasons for the ruination of tribals are their spendthrift manner of marriages and their unfortunate intemperate habits when they go beyond their limits. Any disease or suffering in the tribal family leads to loans from a craftily moneylender who is always watchful of an Adivasi's needs.

With regards to modus operandi of the process of cultivation, forest-cutting commences in early January. It starts at the base of the slope and goes up. The trees, bushes and shrubs are cut in the field itself and piled up in rows. In case of very big trees, however, the trunks are not cut, only the branches are lobbed off. The other trees are cut about eight centimeters above the ground, so as to allow regeneration of the cropping varieties and prevent rapid water and soil run. After these are felled down the branches also are cut into pieces so that these would dry soon land burn better.[5]

After the Jungle is cleared, the trees and the shrubs etc. are allowed for the entire block is done on the same day. The fine is lit with a firetong, metals must not be used. As in the case of cutting, the fire is first starts on the lower side of the slope, so that it can spread upwards.

Different varieties and combination of crops are grown on new fields and old fields. While paddy is sown by the broadcasting method, other crops are grown differently. Small holes are dug by hoe or dao, at distance which differ according to the type of crop and fertility of the soil. Generally these holes dug close to one another, on the spots where larger heaps wood are burnt.[6]

It is further found that weeding operation starts in about the middle of May. A new field requires weeding at least three times, an old field requires weeding at least twice. Richer farmers however undertake weeding in the their fields more frequently.

The poverty stricken tribals generally do not employ labourers on wage basis. A group of friends and relatives combing to form reciprocal labour group, and work in each other's field by turn. On the day work is done on a particular field, the owner of that field is required to serve midday meal to all. Reaping operation is generally conducted on the basis of mutual help. After the date is fixed, a tribal calls his friends and relatives, specially brother-in-law and sister's son to came to his assistance. A pig is killed for the day. Cooking is generally looked after by the sister's husband or sister's son of the owner of the field, while other carry on the reaping and threshing operations.

In shifting cultivation, the main important is attached to the cultivation of food crops like paddy, maize etc. But in order to obtain daily requirements like salt, dry fish, clothes etc. the tribal cultivations also grow some cash crops. Usually the crops are grown in mixture.

Whatever may be methods techniques and stages of shifting cultivation, it is undisputed that shifting cultivation is a positive evil. It is inherently defective, economically unsound and environmentally hazardous. In brief, shifting cultivating is the index on the lack of wisdom in those who resort to it and for those who suffer its continuance even after being aware of its implications.

Agriculture being the backbone of the tribal economy and land being the prized possession in tribal areas shifting cultivation is adopted in the absence of large plain land holdings. In view of the large percentage of tribal cultivators engaged in such ruinous practice of shifting cultivation the adverse effects are to be analysed so as to suggest remedical measures to mitigate the problems arising out of shifting cultivation.

Forests have both physiological and physical effect on the temperature attendant upon the plant growth. The reduce the temperature of the earth because plants transpire water and secondly, because of the Sun's heat is absorbed in the process of evaporation. By reason of its composition living plant substance can not become heated by the sun's rays. It follows that, effect of forests during the growing season is to lower the temperature of the earth and by reducing absorption of heat by earth's surface ti lowers the soil temperature and correspondingly reduces evaporation. Forests not only moderate the intensity of heat in summer as a general rule but also modify the extreme cold of winders. Effects of forests on temperature of a region is highly beneficial to men and animals . By diminishing the velocity wind, forests held to decrease wind erosion. They differ much ameliorate the severity of wind by virtue of physical obstruction they offer.

The shifting cultivator has apparently no idea of the suffering that he is instrumental in causing to the people in the plains below. There being no vegetation cover to consume the rain water, entire rain rushes into the rivers down the slopes of hills ultimately causing devastating flood for the people residing near to the river banks. The rush of the water is so severe and strong that the stream side met lands and terraced lands are sand-cast and changed.

In nutshell, shifting cultivation results in indiscriminate deforestation in large-scale which is followed by soil erosion and the ruination that erosion brings in its wake for vast and rich tracts is a greater ruination.

In view of the detrimental effects associated with shifting cultivation, it must be halted by all means. The key to solve this problem lies with the removal of poverty among the tribals. It has been observed by Dr. Tripathy[8] in his studies made in the tribal district of Phulbani (Orissa) that distressed sale of agricultural produce to the merchants and traders by the tribals caused widespread poverty among the tribals. The cooperatives could able to procure only 10 per cent of the minor forest produce and surplus agricultural produce of the tribals. There is mounting corruption and defective implementation of plans in tribals area. Honesty, sincerity and departmental coordination are lacking in the tribal regions and planned efforts and expenditures are not percolating in tribal districts of Orissa. These are the cumulatively factors responsible for the growing poverty of the tribals. Therefore, the activities of the middlemen, businessmen, traders should be regulated in order to ensure fair and remunerative price to the tribals for their products. Minimum wages should be guaranteed to the tribal agriculturists for their services discharged. The misappropriation of funds and leakages of funds sanctioned for tribal development must be regulated. Awareness, motivation and self-help strategy can go a long way in removing the bottlenecks in the removal of tribal poverty.

The method suggested of solving, the problem of shifting cultivation is by diverting the hill-tribes to settled agriculture.

Because of non-availability of suitable areas for settled cultivation, it becomes difficult to solve the problem. Perennial water-supply through minor-irrigating programmes can facilitate settled cultivation. Supply of fertiliser, supply of seeds and seedlings, agricultural implements, expert advice, irrigation facilities, demonstration farms and incentives for fruit gardens, publicity regarding evils of shifting cultivation etc. can go a long way in mitigating the problem.

Promotion of cottage industries among hill-tribes like silk, cotton, beedi-leaf collection, bamboo works, rope-making, bee-making, beekeeping etc. will supplement their income and improve their living conditions. Tree planting and afforestation programmes cannot only consume soil and environment but also provide employment to the tribals.

Better soil and water management are to be evolved to retard the trend of shifting cultivation practised among tribals. Unless the trend is reversed and problems of tribal farmers are mitigated through a time-bound programme with political commitment and policy makers, the tribal problems will grow in high proportion and endanger the survival of mankind.

In this context, it will be appropriate to mention that a strategy has been evolved to deal with the problem of shifting cultivation. This was an outcome of careful consideration of reports and recommendations of various committees and commissions, namely the National Commission on Agriculture (1976), Working Group. On Tribal Development during the Sixth Plan (Oct. 1980), the National Committee on the Development of Backward Areas (1981), Committee on Forests and Tribals in India (1982), Research highlight on shifting cultivation and its Alternatives of ICAR Research Complex for North Eastern Hill Region, Shillong (1982), the Task force on Shifting Cultivation in India (Oct. 1983), working Group on Development of Scheduled Tribes during the Seventh five year Plan of Ministry of Home Affairs (December 1984) etc.[9]

The strategy for control of shifting cultivation involves an integrated Programme of reclamation and Development of Land for Settlement of shifting cultivators under regular agriculture, animals husbandry, horticulture and forestry.

REFERENCES

1. Mahalingam, S (Dr.), Shifting Cultivation in Andhra Pradesh, *Social Welfare,* March, 1990, P. 17.
2. NCAPR'77, Perspective Plan of Economic Development, Quoted in *"Shifting Cultivation in India. An Overview"*, *Mainstream,* Nov. 26, 1988, P.20.
3. *Ibid.*
4. Tripathy, S.N., *Exploitation of Child Labour in Tribal India,* Daya Publishing House, Delhi (1991), pp. 35-36
5. Burman, B.K. Roy, Shifting Cultivation in India: An Overview, *Mainstream,* November 26, 1988, p.21.
6. *Ibid.*
7. *Ibid,* p. 22.
8. Tripathy, S.N., *Bonded Labour in India,* Discovery Publishing House, New Delhi, 1989.
9. Verma, R.C., *Indian Tribes Through the Ages.,* Publications Division, Ministry of Information & Broadcasting, Govt. of India, 1990.

10

Problems of Displacement and Development*

The important aims of river dam projects were controlling floods, generating electricity and providing facilities of irrigation. During last one hundred years, there were 4291 large river dam projects started. Because of these river dam projects about 11.5 crores of people have been displaced. According to Central Water Commission at an average 24,535 hectares of land have been submerged by water by 54 river dam projects. According to Indian Institute of Public Administration—which collected data on 213 river dam projects reveals that per each river dam project at an average 8,748 hectares of land have been displaced by these 213 river dam projects. The data collected form 34 river dam projects reveal the fact that out of displaced people 47% are tribals. The volume of displaced people by all type of developmental projects are much higher than river projects. According to the World Refugee Survey (2000) the magnitude of industrially displacement of people in India was 5,07,000 whereas the Indian Social Institute, New Delhi estimated total as 21.3 million, out of which displaced due to dams constitute 16.4 million, mines 2.55 million, Industrial development 1.25 million, Wildlife sanctuaries 7 million and National Park 0.6 million (Fernandes, 1994).[1]

*Also published in the book, *Economic Development and Problems of Displacement*, Anmol, New Delhi.

The number of population displaced by different developmental projects in India since the commencement of five year plan till 1990 stood at around 1.85 crs. (Table 1).

Table 1
Displacement of Population by Development Projects (1981-90)

S.No.	Projects	Number of Projects	Year	Displaced Population
1.	Large Dams	2422	1990	1,40,000.00
2.	Mines	1210	1983	21,000.00
3.	Industries	—	1990	13,000.00
4.	Parks & Sanctuary	468	1990	6,000.00
5.	Others	—	—	5,000.00
	Total			1,85,000.00

Source: Development, Displacement and Rehabilitation in Tribal Areas of Orissa (1992), Indian Social Institute, New Delhi.

According to the World Commission on Dams (WCD) by India Country Study (ICS), during 1980 to 2000, the major river dams have submerged 91 lakh hectars of forests.

Table 2 demonstrates the displaced population as well as the tribal displaced population due to the river dam projects in India.

It is found that the displaced population was 15,000 during 1979 which increased to two lakh twenty thousand by 1995. About 90% of displaced people in various dam projects have not been provided justice. During last 50 years, in various dams about 6 crores of population have been displaced. Out of these 6 crores, 4 crores have virtually become beggars in the street. On the contrary, despite these dams, due to improper utilization of dam water only 10% of agricultural land of India could yield crops.

The Narmada Valley Project (NVP) is the largest multipurpose river project in India. The NVP aims to provide water to the drought prone districts of Sourastra, Kutch, North Gujarat and some parts of Rajasthan. At 1988 base index, the NVP will cost the exchequer about Rs. 5000 crores and displace about over 1 million people. It will submerge over 37,000 hectares of land. It will cause a loss of standing forests over worth Rs. 30,000 crores. In this context is mention-worthy that, "In a majority decision, with tow judges including the Chief Justice of India in favour of the Narmada Project and one member of the Apex Court dissenting, the Supreme Court has ruled that construction work on the dam up to a height of 90 meters be taken up immediately."

Table 2
River Dam Projects and Displaced Population

Projects	State	Displaced Population	Displaced Tribal People
01	02	03	04
Curzen	Gujarat	11,600	100%
Sardar Sarovar	Gujarat	2,00,000	57.06%
Maheswar	Madhya Pradesh	20,000	60%
Dhabaghat	Madhya Pradesh	13,000	73.91%
Ichha	Bihar	30,800	80%
Chandil	Bihar	37,600	87%
Koelkar	Bihar	66,000	88%
Mohibajaj Sagar	Rajasthan	38,400	76.28%
Polbharam	Andhra Pradesh	1,50,000	52.90%
Mythan	Bihar	93,870	56.46%
Upper Indravati	Orissa	18,500	89.20%
Ichhampali	Himachal Pradesh	38,100	76.28%
Tultil	Andhra Pradesh	13,600	51.61%
Domanganga	Gujarat	8,7000	48.70%
Bhakra	Himachal Pradesh	36,000	34.36%
Manas	Bihar	3,700	31.00%
Bhalkar	Gujarat	52,000	18.92%

Source: The Pragatibadi, The Oriya Daily, Dated 27.12.2000

Significantly, the reason for clearance of the Project is based on the Court's satisfaction at the manner in which the relief and rehabilitation of these ousted by the dam are being undertaken. This is the one issue of which the Narmada Bachao Andolan (NBA) has created a countrywide movement, drawing attention of the misery and plight of those displaced so far and these likely to be ousted with the planned increase in the height of the structure (The Times of India, 14.11.2000).

The NBA needs to be congratulated for bringing to public attention an issue which has generally been neglected in the pat while implementing many public or private sector projects. It has been manifested that some ousted families were constrained to move as many as six times. This is a cruel state of affair on the significance we attention we attach to the human dimension of a problem.

The most negative impact of Narmada Dam Project will be felt by Madhya Pradesh, which would have to rehabilitate the largest number of person likely to be displaced. The power generation from the Narmada Dam Project would hardly be significant with a capacity of 1,450 MW.

In this context, Pachauri (2000)[2] has aptly remarked, "If indeed the only means of getting water in areas of Gujarat and Rajasthan that are chronically water scarce is through this Project, then what weight age due are attach to this benefits vis-a-vis the acute misery of being ousted in Madhya Pradesh? There is clearly a case of uneven costs and benefits to which there are no simple answers, and hence the sharply divergent position on the subject between Gujarat and Madhya Pradesh."

Development Induced Displacement in Orissa

According to official estimates the total number of families displaced due to river dam projects and other development projects in Orissa between 1950-1993 was 81,176 of which 80 per cent families have been displaced due to irrigation projects only (Pandey, 2000)[3]. During the said period mining activities have displaced 3,145 thousands, industries, 10,704, thermal power 2,426 and dams 64,903. In a official estimate only Hirakud mam has displaced around 40 thousand people, but other study demonstrate the number of displaced persons over 180 thousand. The picture relating to displaced families due to various development project in Orissa can be found from the Table 3.

Table 3

S.No.	Name of the Project	Displaced Families	ST/SC Families
1.	Balimela Multipurpose dam project on Sileru river at Chitrakonda.	2000	
2.	Salandi Irrigation Project	589	552 tribals families.
3.	Rengali Multipurpose river valley project on the Brahmani river in Angul District.	10,897	1,710 SC families. 1172 ST families.
4.	Upper Kolab Multipurpose dam project on the river Kolab in Koraput District.	3,179	442 SC families 1421 ST families.
5.	Upper Indravati Multi-purpose project.	5,301	2223 families Tribals 796 families SC.
6.	Talcher Steel Plant.	4,251	—
7.	Talcher Coal belt region in Angul District.	23 villages affected by underground mines due to open cast miningproject 38 villages.	
8.	IB valley area in Jharsuguda District.	17 villages affected and 130 families displaceddue to five open cast mining.	—

*Source: Pandey, Balaji (1998), Depriving the underprivileged by Development, Bhubaneshwar.

Problem involved in Compensation Payment

Displacement because of long-term projects, like construction of a reservoir, power plant, industry and mining may take over an area displacing the inhabitants. This involuntary displacement or development induced displacement with a view to achieve accelerated economic development through various investment projects necessitates vast amount of land. This land acquisition for public interest and national building are made through the payment of compensation to the owner of land or housing property etc.

Prof. G.C. Kar (1999)[4] remarks, "When ownership rights become the only point in determining compensation then three disadvantageous situations may arise:

1. What about those who do not own land individually? In many tribal communities land is held by the community families are given the right to cultivate. The arrangement is oral-between the tribal Chief and the family and, no record is maintained.

2. What about those do not own land either individually or as a community but depend on land for a living? The landless agricultural laborers belong to this category.

3. What about those who are no land owners and yet cultivate land? Tenants and sub-tenants belong to this category."

The aforesaid issues are not taken into account while compensating the displaced persons. Moreover, compensation for land acquisition is indicated as an element of total project cost. But in fact, displacement involves several other type of sasts risk like (i) Landlessness (ii) Joblessness (iii) Homelessness (iv) Marginalisation (v) Increased morbidity (vi) Food insecurity (vii) Less of access to common property etc.

Multiple Displacement

Because of displacement, the oustees undergo an acute psychological, physical economic trauma as well as identity crisis. The oustees face untold problems due to multiple displacement. The inhuman tragedy and plight of oustees of Hindustan Aeronautics Limited (HAL), Hirakud Dam Project, can be well conceived as illustrations of this Multiple displacement. The HAL oustees displaced during 1960s second time due to Upper Kolab Multipurpose Dam Project. The Rihand Dam oustees were displaced first by the dam itself, then by coal mines, then again by thermal plants and finally when the government declared their colony was forest land. Similarly, the oustees of Hirakud Dam Project who were displaced in the mid-1950s and resettled in Brajarajnagar area of Jharsuguda district, confronted displacement for the second time because of construction of the Ib Thermal Power Station in the late 1980s.

Though the development of economy and the region is intended by such dam projects and other developmental projects, but acute problems have been caused especially tribals, small farmers and marginal farmers.

It is inferred form the analysis that the development projects and river dam projects restricted the community right over natural resources, rich forest areas have been exploited and tribal inhabitants and original habitants of the project area have been vulnerable to explcitation and pauperization.

In this context it is imperative that the NGO should play an active role in mobilizing people and tribals to protect the resources, habitant and the tribals, and must actively cooperate in their resettlement programmes. The rehabilitation programme should be genuine, just and must minimise the suffering of the people.

REFERENCES

1. Fernandes, W. (1994): *Development induced Displacement in the Tribal Areas of Eastern India*, New Delhi, Indian Social Institute (Mimeo).
2. Pachauri, R.K. (2000), Might of Contention (A Damed Model of Development), *The Times of India*, 17th November.
3. Pandey, Balaji (2000), Protection of right to livelihood and survival of the development induced displaced persons in Orissa: A note for discussion, *Vision* (Vol. XIX. Nos. 3-4), pp. 94-95.
4. Kar, G.C. (1999), Displacement, Resettlement and Rehabilitation, *Orissa Economic Journal*, Vol. XXXI, No. 1 & 2, p. 19.

11

Role of LAMPS for the Development of Tribals in Orissa*

As per 1991 census, Orissa has more than 70.32 lakh tribal population constituting 22.21 percent of the total population. It is found from various census reports that though in terms of absolute numbers the tribal population has been increasing, but the percentage of tribals to total population of the State has been decreasing from 24.07 percent in 1961 to 23.11 percent in 1971 and to 22.43 percent in 1981 which finally to 22.31 percent in 1991, (Table 11.1). The undivided districts of Koraput, Mayurbhanj, Sundargarh, Kalahandi and Phulbani are mostly tribal concentrated.

Table 11.1
Percentage of Tribal Population in Orissa as per Various Census Reports

Census Year	Total Population	Tribal Population	Percentage of Tribal Population to the total population
1961	17,548,846	42,23,757	24.07
1971	21,944,615	50,71,937	23.11
1981	26,370,271	59,15,067	22.43
1991	31,659,736	70,32,214	22.21

Source: Collected from various Census Reports

* Also published in the book, *'Cooperatives: Its Growth and New Dimensions'*.

There are 62 types of tribes in Orissa, residing in the remote areas of forests, hills and naturally isolated regions. Most of he tribals in Orissa are much below the poverty line and thus, in the state of backwardness. These tribals perform a wide spectrum of activities ranging from food gathering and hunting to slash and burn cultivation (Podu or shifting cultivation), settled plough cultivation with occasional practices of cottage industries. The tribals of Orissa, with slight variations have a highly egalitarian society, with high status for women and dignity of labour. They have maintained their values as manifested in their rites, rituals and traditionals institutions, in spite of centuries of on slaught by external forces.

The Tribal Problems

Tribals in India, as well as Orissa, have been experiencing diverse problems. Taking the advantage of their illiteracy, simplicity and ignorance, and the moneylenders, the middlemen and of the unscrupulous traders enter into the tribal regions and exploit then through various dubious means. Besides, they also con from the problem of land alienation, exorbitant rate of interest, wide spread poverty and indebtedness, bondage, exploitation, leading to sale of child and starvation death.

These miseries of tribals accentuate due to rapid growth of population, pressure on landholding, illiteracy, deforestation, inadequate infrastructural and social service facilities etc. Even some of the tribals are uprooted form their native abodes either due to displacement by non-tribals or due to establishment of major industrial and irrigation projects.

Cooperative Approach for Tribal Development

To eliminate the age old exploitation and repression of tribals in different economic activities, sincere efforts have been made by the Government in building up cooperative structure in the tribal economy during the plan period in India. Many commissions, committees, study teams and working groups have repeatedly been emphasised the significance of cooperativization of tribal economy in the country. In its report, the social welfare team of the committee on plan projects (1959) recommended that, "Commercial exploitation of forests be entrusted to cooperatives rather than to contractors." The Dhebar Commission

(1961) recommended that "the sale and marketing of the produce and supply of trial peoples' requirements at reasonable price should receive special attention through cooperatives. A special working group on Cooperation (1961) attributed the slow development of Cooperative movement in tribal areas to structural defects, management problems, faulty procedures and business methods. The group suggested a separate organizational set up for promotion of cooperative ideas among the tribal communities, so as to provide such service as were being rendered by private traders and further, recommended the formation of an "Integrated service Cooperative societies and multipurpose cooperative societies and State Level Tribal Development Corporations. Further, to improve the operational efficiency of cooperatives in Tribal Areas, Committee on cooperative structure in Tribal Areas under the Chairmanship of K.S. Bawa (1971) has recommended for the Chairmanship of the Large Scale Adivasi Multipurpose Societies (LAMPS) by amalgamating service coop. Societies (SCS) in tribal areas which include package of service for tribal people. The main components of this package are credit (both production and consumption), supply of seeds and other agricultural inputs, marketing of agricultural and minor forest produce and supply of consumer goods. The committee recommended that a tribesman should not be required to approach too many institutions for assistance and the cooperative structure should essentially provide integrated credit and other services at one point. They suggested for creation of LAMPS at block level with branches at G.P. Head quarters or at important weekly market/Haat centres. Fore credit purposes the LAMPS have to be serviced by the Central Cooperative Banks (CCB), for supply of inputs and marketing and agricultural produce to the Regional Cooperative Marketing Society (RCMS) and for marketing of minor forest produce (MFP) to the Triabl Development Cooperative Society.

A detailed picture of the membership covered by LAMPS in Orissa during the period 1989-90 to 1994-95 has been presented in the Table 11.2. It is revealed from the table that the membership of the LAMPS in Orissa has increased form 808 thousands to 906 thousand during the said period. The participation of tribals in the total membership is about 58 percent.

Credit Flow

Credit is an essential input for the development of tribal agriculture. The LAMPS supply short terms and medium terms loans for agricultural purposes alongwith some amount of consumption loans.

Table 11.2

Statement Showing Membership of LAMPS in Orissa

Year	No. of LAMPS	Membership (in thousand) ST	SC	Others	Total Membership
1989-90	223	472 (58.41)	116	220	808
1990-91	223	482 (57.43)	120	230	832
1991-92	223	510 (57.73)	127	238	875
1993-94	223	512 (57.65)	130	246	888
1994-95	223	519 (57.28)	132	255	906

Source: Collected from various Census Reports.

Table 11.3

The Advancement of Loans by LAMPS in Orissa

(*Rs. in Lakhs*)

Year	Short-term Loans	Medium-term Loans	Total loan Outstanding
1989-90	273 (7.54)	30 (0.82)	3617
1990-91	541 (23.46)	8 (0.34)	2306
1991-92	466 (25.28)	71 (3.85)	1843
1992-93	719 (35.75)	166 (8.25)	2011
1993-94	1084 (46.32)	495 (19.87)	2340
1994-95	1359 (47.88)	440 (15.64)	2838

Source: Office of the R.C.S., Orissa, Bhubaneswar

The detailed position regarding the advancement of loans by LAMPS has been exhibited in the Table 11.3. It is depicted from the Table that the percentage of shot-term loans during the period 1989-90 to 1994-95 marks an increasing trend. It has increased 7.54 percent to 47.88 period during the said period. Similarly, the flow of medium-term loans shows an increasing trend as it has registered a sharp rise from 0.82 percent in the 1989-90 to 1991-92. However, from 1992-93 onwards it registers a rising trend. The probable reason for increasing total outstanding loans during the said period may be due to non repayment of loans because of failure of crops, natural calamities and lack of employment.

Further, the position of total loans overdue reveals a disheartening picture (Table 11.4). The scheduled castes and schedule tribes combinedly held approximately more that 50 percent of the loans. Exclusively, the tribals held about 40 percent of loans overdue. This speaks in volumes about the magnitude of poverty prevailing in the tribal areas.

Table 11.4
Position of Loans Overdue
(Both Short-term and Medium-term Loans)

Year	Total Loan Overdue	Total ST + SC Loan Overdue	Loans Overdue by ST	Loans Overdue by SC
1989-90	2592	1429 (55.13)	1103 (42.55)	326 (12.57)
1990-91	1449	823 (56.79)	625 (43.13)	198 (13.66)
1991-92	1209	627 (55.91)	517 (42.76)	159 (13.15)
1992-93	1321	597 (45.19)	416 (31.49)	181 (13.57)
1994-95	1431	761 (53.17)	577 (40.32)	184 (12.85)

Source: Office of the R.C.S., Orissa, Bhubaneswar.

Note: Figures in the parenthesis indicate the percentage to the total.

It is found from the Table 11.5 that there has been fluctuation in collection of tribal agricultural produce by the LAMPS. Generally the tribals who are in the grip of unemployment and poverty, borrow from the moneylenders and businessmen in order to meet their urgent needs. Therefore, they are compelled to sale their products at a distressed price to such unscrupulous traders and middlemen. The value of Agricultural produce marketed by LAMPS in the year 1991-92 was as high as Rs. 774 lakhs. The important agricultural produces procured by LAMPS are maize, Jowar, Ragi, Blackgram, Mustard seeds, Niger seeds etc.

Table 11.5
Marketing of Surplus Agricultural Produce (SAP) through LAMPS in Orissa

(Rs. in Lakhs)

Year	Agricultural produce marked
1989-90	54
1990-91	371
1991-92	774
1992-93	251
1993-94	62
1994-95	121

Source: As stated in Table 11.4.

However, with regard to marketing of agricultural produces of tribals, the LAMPS fail to procure the produce adequately from them as the tribals apprehend the adjustment of their agricultural produce towards their loan overdues. Therefore, it has been observed that the private traders and middlemen could procure more than eighty percent of the tribal agricultural produce and thereby exploit the tribals though distressed payment.

A perusal of the aforesaid analysis brings to light that even though the LAMPS have played a vital role in the advancement of credit cum marketing of products, it is indispensable to bring the tribals under cooperative fold for relieving them from the clutches of the private money lenders-Cum-traders. Because of the tribals fail to receive a fair and remunerative return for their products and if the exploitative elements continue to deny them the fruits of their labour, mere increase of the financial resources in five year plans for tribal welfare and execution of tribal development programmes may not benefit them to the extent contemplated. Therefore, there should be a proper coordination of institutional agencies like Agency marketing cooperative society, Tribal Development Cooperative corporations, State Marketing Federation etc. through supply of money to LAMPS. The tribal development strategy should be an integrated strategy combing the development of credit-Cum-Marketing facilities, infrastructural development, development of education, removal of exploitation of middlemen through payment of support prices to the tribals, provision of adequate employment and finally, to the active involvement of tribals in the process of development.

REFERENCES

1. Tripathy, S.N., *Marketing Cooperatives for Tribal Development, Social Welfare*, November, 1998.
2. Tripathy, S.N., *Bonded Labour in India*, Discovery Publishing House, New Delhi, 1989.
3. Tripathy, S.N., *Impact of Road Transport in Tribal India*, Discovery Publishing House, New Delhi, 1994.
4. Tripathy, S.N., *Cooperatives for Rural Development*, Discovery Publishing House, New Delhi, 1998.

12

Evaluating Women Self-Help Groups in Tribal Orissa

The tribal population constitute about 8.8 percent of the population of India. Next to Madhya Pradesh, Orissa has the largest concentration of tribal population in India. There are 62 tribes in Orissa with the population of 72.32 Lakhs as per 1991 census constituting about 22.2 percent of the total population of State.

The backwardness of the tribal regions, widespread poverty of the tribals and problems of integrating them with the mainstream of civilisation etc., are the stumbling-blocks in the path of tribal development. Thus, the tribals in Orissa continued to remain socially, economically and educationally backward and are languishing at the bottom of the socioeconomic ladder. For generation together they are residing in inaccessible forest and hilly areas. Their geographical isolation and improverished economy have made them object of exploitative economic and trade practices of non-tribal living or entering areas. The powerful exgenious forces of money lenders, contractors, officials having their link with political personnel and police could exert dominant control and gratify the selfish greed of exploiting the tribals. The poverty stricken, illiterate, innocent, simple tribals fail to withstand the counterveiling exgenious forces and becoming prey to all types of exploitation.

Role of Intervening Agencies—Self Help Groups (SHGs)

Despite the vast expansion of the formal credit system in India, the dependence of the rural poor on money, lenders, continues in some areas especially for meeting emergent credit requirements. Such dependencies pronounced in the case of marginal farmers, landless labourers, petty traders and rural artisans belonging to the socially and economically backward classes and the tribal population particularly in the resource-poor areas.

For various reasons the credit flow to these sections of the population for meeting their full credit requirements has not come to be institutionalised. Some of the major causes lie in the difficulties in dealing effectively and economically with a large number of small borrowers, who require credit frequently and in small quantities, limitations imposed by the legal framework on their operations and also due to the Bank's perceptions of the risks and credit worthiness of these borrowers.

The credit needs of the rural poor are determined in a complex socioeconomic milieu, where it is difficult to adopt project lending approach as followed by banks and where the dividing line between credit for "consumption" and "Productive" purpose is blurred. Under the circumstances, a non-formal agency of credit supply to the poor, in the form of "Self Help Group" of the poor could emerge as a promising partner of the formal agencies. In many instances the poor have demonstrated their potential for self-help to secure greater economic and financial strength and many such self-help groups have come into existence spontaneously or with the active involvement of voluntary agencies or official development agencies. Such SHGs have been formed generally around specific issues confronting the poor or specific production activities and often they have mobilised saving among their members, who would normally not be expected to have any savings and used such resources to meet emergent credit needs of members of the group. The demonstratic functioning of the successful SHGs, their adroitness in assessing and appraising the credit needs of members, their business like functioning and efficiency in recycling the funds often with repayment rates nearing cent percent, are additional welcome features that the bankers may like to utilise for serving the credit needs of the poor.

A recognition by the formal credit structure of the self-management capabilities of the poor through the SHGs and a link up between the two is expected result in specific advantages to both the systems. Under the linkage project, the main advantages to both the systems. Under the linkage project, the main advantages to the banks would be externalisation of part of the work items of the credit cycle-assessment of credit needs, appraisal, disbursal, supervision and repayment-reduction in the formal paper work involved and a consequent reduction in the formal paper work involved and a consequent reduction in the transaction costs. Improvement in recoveries and also in the margins would lead a wider coverage of the target group. A large mobilisation of small savings would be equally advantageous. For the groups, the advantages lie in the access to a larger quantum of resources as compared to their meagre corpus generated through thrift, access to better technology and skill upgradation through different schemes of the Banking sector and a general improvement in the nature and scale of operation that would accelerate economic development.

In this backdrop, let us highlight the women SHGs in Orissa and particularly in the tribal districts of Orissa.

Women SHGs

It has been conceived that the objective of eradicating poverty cannot be achieved without the active participation of women in the process of development. Women led Self-Help Group (SHGs) as a medium of micro-finance is gaining momentum in the endeavour to alleviate poverty of the marginalized sections and tribals.

In the state of Orissa, 49.72 percent of the population belong to poverty section as per National Sample Survey Organisation estimated as against 37.27 percent of all India average. The females constitute 49.26 percent of the State population of 31.66 lakhs, who are the vulnerable sections in he realm of health, education and economic independence. In the context of tribal women who are illiterate and their credit needs are not adequately met by formal financial institutions in the country despite a vast network of financial institutions. It is therefore, imperative to focus light on the women SHG in the tribal districts of Orissa.

Objectives of the Study

1. To outline the activities and functioning of Groups in terms of their operations, activities, strategies, problems and future perspectives.
2. To present the need and the dimension of linkage of SHGs with banks/financial institutions.
3. To examine the role of SHGs in sample tribal dominated districts of Orissa in ameliorating the socioeconomic conditions of tribal women.

Methodology

This research write-up is based on primary as well as secondary sources of data. The Self-Help Promoting Institutions (SHPIs) who play catalystic role in promoting SHGs have been enlisted to select viable SHGs. A total of 60 women SHGs have been selected with the help of stratified random sampling. As there are a series of SHGs working in the state for promoting SHGs, thus, each SHIP is considerable as one stratum.

Twenty women SHGs have been randomly selected from each tribal dominated districts of Kandhamal, Kalahandi and Raygada for the purpose of study. Twenty SHGs promoted by leading SHPI in each district aggregating 60 SHGs in all the three tribal districts have been selected for analysis of data required for the study.

Further, two members from each SHG have been purposively selected on the basis of maximum amount of loans received and savings made.

Features of Women SHGs

The districts and community-wise distribution of sample SHGs have been presented in Table 12.1. A uniform number of

8 tribal SHGs from each districts under review have been selected and from General caste category 12 number of SHGs from each district have been selected. Thus, 24 tribals SHGs, 36 general SHGs aggregating 60 SHGs and 120 group members have been selected for analysis.

Table 12.1
District and Community-wise Distribution of SHGs

Sample Districts	Scheduled Tribe	General	SHPIs
Kandhamals	8	12	1) Samanmita 2) Nehru Yuva Kendra
Kalahandi	8	12	1) Indira Manila Yojana 2) Swarna Jayanti Gram Swarojgar Yonana (SGSY)
Rayagada	8	12	1) Panchabati Gramya Bank 2) Vikas Nikatan
Total	24	36	
Percentage	40%	60%	

Table 12.2 depicts the Self-Help Promoting Institutions which set up SHGs in the three districts in our study. We have taken the highest number of 15 SHGs (25%) promoted by Nehru Yuva Kendra, followed by 14 SHGs (23.33%) promoted by Panchabati Gramya Bank.

Table 12.2
Distribution of SHGs as Per Their Respective SHPIs

Self-Help Promoting Institutions (SHPIs)	Number of SHGs	Percentage
Samanmita (NGO)	5	8.33
Vikas Niketan (NGO)	6	10.00
Indira Mahila Yojana	8	13.33
Panchabati Gramya Bank	14	23.33
Nehru Yuva Kendra	15	25.00
SGSY	12	20.00
Total	60	100.00

Table 12.3
Group Structure According to the Size of Some SHGs

Size of the Group	No. of SHGs	Percentage
Less than 10 members	18	30.00
10-15 members	27	45.00
15-25 members	15	25.00
	60	100.00

Table 12.3 presents group structure of SHGs according to their size. SHG within 10 to 15 members constitute the highest percentage 45 percent, followed by less than 10 members Self-Help Group (30%). There are 15SHGs in the membership size of 15-25 (25%) in our study.

Table 12.4
Socio-Economic Profile of the Group Members

Socioeconomic Profile	No. of members	Percentage
Occupational Structure		
Agriculture	42	35
Allied activities (Dairy, Fishery, Others)	16	13.33
Collection of Minor Forest Product	24	20.00
Household industry/Crafts	4	3.33
Business	14	11.66
Labour/wage earning	20	16.67
Total	120	100%
Age Group		
18-30	55	45.83
30-45	18	15.00
35-40	27	22.50
40 and above	20	16.66
Total	120	100%
Level of Literacy		
Illiterate	29	24.16
Knowing only signature	76	63.33
Read and write	15	12.50
Total	120	100%
Marital Status		
Married	85	70.83
Unmarried	35	29.16
Total	120	100%

Table 12.4 demonstrates the socioeconomic profile of the Group Members. It is found from the table that 42 members constituting 35 percent have agriculture as their occupation followed by 24 members (20%), who have the main occupation of collecting minor forest produce. Labour or wage earning the chief source of occupation for 20 members which is 16.67 percent of the total. The SHG members were mostly in the age-group of 18 to 30 (45.83%) within the age group of 30 to 45, there were 18 members (15%) within the age group of 35 to 40, there were 27 members constituting 22.50 percent of the total SHG members.

Table 12.5.
Frequency of Group Meetings

Frequency of the Group meetings	No. of SHGs	Percentage
Weekly	2	(3.33)
Monthly	38	(63.33)
Quaterly	12	(20.00)
Frequently	8	(13.33)
Total	60	(100%)

(Percentage in the brackets represents to the total).

The study further reveals that 85 members constituting 70.83% are married and rest are unmarried.

The literacy position shows that 76 members (63.35%) only aware of putting their signature and 15 members (12.5%) can read and write.

The Group Meetings were mostly conducted on monthly basis (63.33%) followed quarterly basis (20.00%). Only 2 SHGs reported about the weekly conduct of meeting which comes to 3.33 percent of the total.

Table 12.6 depicts the amount of loans available by the SHGs. There were 25 number of SHGs (41.66%) who availed loan in the range of Rs. 10,000 and above. Loans in the range of Rs. 5,000-10,000 have been available by 20 SHGs (33.33%). Loans upto 5,000 have been availed by 15 numbers of SHGs constituting 25.00% of the total SHGs studied.

Table 12.6
Loans Available by the SHGs

Range	No. of SHGs	Percentage
Upto 5,000	15	(25.00)
5,001-10,000	20	(33.33)
10,001 and above	25	(41.66)
Total	60	(100.00)

Table 12.7 reveals the position of average monthly income generated by the SHGs. Out of 60 SHGs studied, 34 SHGs (56.66%) generated income in the range of Rs. 501-1,000. There were 8 SHGs, generating monthly income of Rs. 1,001 and above (13.33%).

Table 12.7
Distribution of SHGs According to Average Monthly Income

Average income Generated	No. of SHGs	Percentage
Upto Rs. 500	18	(30.00)
Rs.501-1000	34	(56.66)
Rs. 1001 and above	08	(13.33)
Total	60	(100.00)

Table 12.8 presents the reasons for the formation of SHGs. The highest number of 28 SHGs (46.67) were formed with a view of receiving economic benefits followed by 10 SHGs for upgradation of traditional occupation (16.66%).

Table 12.8.
Reasons for the Formation of SHGs

Reason	No. of SHGs	Percentage
Social Factors	8	(13.33)
Economic Benefits	28	(46.67)
Debt Burden	6	(10.00)
Upgradation of Traditional Occupation	10	(16.66)
Others	8	(13.33)
Total	60	100%

Table 12.9 demonstrates the monthly saving position of women members in the SHGs studied. It is revealed that women members in 25 SHGs (41.66%) could save monthly in the range of Rs. 1.61-91. Only 8 SHGs (13.33%) reported about their monthly saving about Rs. 91/-.

Table 12.9
Monthly Savings of Women Members in SHGs

Savings (Rs.)	No. of SHGs	Percentage
10-30	7	(11.66)
31-60	20	(33.33)
61-91	25	(41.66)
91+	8	(13.33)
Total	60	(100%)

Table 12.10 depicts the distribution of SHGs according to frequently of loans. Out of 60 SHGs, 25 SHG members (41.66%) reported that they have availed loan for the third time in a year. Twenty-two SHG members (36.66%) reported that during the last year they have availed loan twice, number of 7 SHGs (11.67% of the total) have reported regarding their acceptance of loan fourth time in a year.

Table 12.10
Distribution of SHGs According to Frequency of Loans (in a year)

Frequency	No. of SHGs	Percentage
First time	5	(8.33)
Second time	22	(36.66)
Third time	25	(41.66)
Fourth time	7	(11.67)
Not availed	1	(1.67)
Total	60	100%

Table 12.11. unfolds the loan utilisation pattern of the members in SHGs under study. It is seen from the table that 28 SHGs constituting 46.66 percent mostly utilise the loan for consumption purposes in the tribal; dominated districts of Orissa. However, 24 SHGs (40%) reported that they have utilised the loan for agricultural development purposes.

Table 12.11
Loan Utilisation of Women Members in SHGs

Utilisation	No. of SHGs	Percentage
Agriculture	24	(40.00)
Consumption	28	(46.66)
Entrepreneur	5	(8.33)
Others (Marriage, health etc.)	2	(3.33)
No loan		
Total	60	(100%)

Table 12.12
Profile of the Selected Study Districts

Particulars	Unit	Kandhamal	Kalahandi	Rayagada
Geographical Area	Kms	7650	8364	7580
Sub-Divisions	Nos	2	2	2
Tahsils	Nos	4	7	4
CD Block	Nos	12	13	11
Gram Panchayats	Nos	144	195	140
Villages	Nos	2515	2205	2667
(i) Inhabited	Nos	2336	2068	2445
(ii) Uninhabited	Nos	179	137	222
Total Population	Nos	546	1131	714
Male Population	Nos	273	566	355
Female Population	Nos	273	565	359
Sex-Ratio (Female per 1000 males)	Figure	999	999	1012
Percentage of ST Population to the District total Population	Figure	51.5	28.0	56.0

Source. District Statistical Hand Books, Govt. of Orissa.

Empowerment

The basic objectives of the policies, intervention programmes, enactments and institutions are to bring the marginalised, poor tribes into the mainstream of development by making them self-reliant. The institutional support through the flow of micro-credit organised and implemented, via: SHGs in tribal dominated districts of Kandhamal, Kalahandi and Rayagada which constitute the regions under the most backward KBK districts of Orissa, have certainly accelerated in creating a better impact on the quality of life of tribals. In fact, the dynamics of SHG programme to develop the socially and economically disadvantaged groups have definitely enhanced their capability, made them self-dependent and interdependent and ultimately paved the way of waging a crusade against the age-old expatiation of money lenders and traders in tribal areas.

13

Tribal Migration: A Study in KBK Districts of Orissa*

Normally migration of labourers from rural to urban areas has been viewed as an economic phenomenon, even though non-economic factors have some bearing. Primarily due to lack of employment in their area of origin, migration occurs in order to provide better scope to the migrants elsewhere. With the growth of urbanisation and industrialization, the trend of migration within the country has increased significantly.

However, in the context of Orissa, the plights and problems of migrant labourers have caught the attention of the researchers, social workers and media personalities.

Despite deep concern over the issue of migrant labour, no reliable data are available with regard to magnitude and size of the migrant workmen in the state of Orissa. More than two decades ago during 1988 on the basis of complaints received, investigations made and enquiries conducted by the Labour Directorate, Orissa, estimate the size of migrant labour from Orissa at about 1.5 lakhs every year. But the incidence of migrant labour in Orissa is vast and extensive as it embraces various categories of migrant labour including Surat and other migrants.

*Paper presented in the national consultation on PESA Act (18-19, January 2005), organised by AGRAGAMEE, Kashmir Orissa.

In fact, out-migration of rural workmen is not a recent phenomenon. It is found not only in the coastal districts but also in the poverty-stricken tribal districts of Kalahandi, Bolangir and Koraput (the undivided KBK) districts of Orissa. Rural workers cross the boundaries of the state of Raipur, Ichapuram, and Visakhapatman after the kharif season every year. There were also cases of inter-district move out of labourers with their families to the coastal districts of Ganjam, Puri and Cuttak districts though agents/Khatadars and contractors to different brick-kilns, Even interstate migration of labourers to Andhra Pradesh, Chatishgarh and orchards of Madhya Pradesh has been observed over the last two decades.

In the context of economic analysis, the characteristics of migrant workmen are: (i) seasonal employment of labour; (ii) recruitment through a contractor; (iii) not necessarily landless labours but marginal farmers as they return to their native land in the monsoon and leave the native/land after kharif harvest; and (iv) exploited by agents, cheated by contractors, and employers.

The phenomenon of rural-urban migration, must be viewed in the light of prevailing rural conditions of poverty, inequality, unemployment which the Government policy of rural development could not mitigate due to leakages of funds, misappropriation and other factors. Thus, the problem of rural-urban migration has its ramification in the totality of the problem of poverty and unemployment.

With the state's economy hitting the lowest ebb and job market going dry, the labour migration has assumed alarming proportion, particularly in the tribal dominated districts. Though the famished labourers travel to far off placed in search of livelihood, their financial condition hardly improves, as they become easy targets of exploitation by the employers outside the state.

Unable to find a source of living in their native places, the tribal youths have migrated to developed states like Andhra Pradesh, Gujarat, Karnataka as well as relatively less prosperous one including Chattisgarh, Rajasthan and Meghalaya (The new Indian Express, November 6, 2003, P.6)

In the absence of a detailed study, the present study has been claimed to be the first such study ever attempted confined to Kalahandi, Bolangir and Malkanagiri the drought prone, tribal dominated and backward districts of Orissa.

The Study in general and the regional analysis in particular, provides a necessary base for further research into the underlying reasons of tribal migration and its socioeconomic consequences.

Coverage and Methodology

The present study has been mainly confined to migrants of tribal concentrated sample villages of Kalahandi, Bolangir and Malkanagiri—the poverty stricken; drought ravaged tribal dominated districts of Orissa. These three districts have been selected, as these districts are the most backward districts in the country known as KBK districts.

However, though the filed analysis has been on the sample tribal dominated villages of these districts, but the overall work has been developed on the basis of general framework and in-depth study of various issues relating to rural-urban migration in the State of Orissa with the help of both primary and secondary sources of available data.

Keeping in view the constraints of time and cost, it was decided to collect field data for the present study from 6 blocks. Two blocks from each sample district have been randomly selected for the purpose of field study. First of all a list of the blocks falling in the selected districts has been prepared. From among the blocks, two blocks named Kesinga and Dharamgarh blocks in Kalahandi districts, Belpara and Turekala block in Bolangir district and Kudumulugumma and Kalimela block in Malkanagiri district have been selected on the basis of their tribal concentration, migration potentiality and accessibility. After selection of the blocks have been made, the list of villages be identified for field studies on the basis of tribal concentration. After the list of tribal villages has been prepared, 3 villages in each block have been selected through random sampling method. Thus, all total 18 villages have been covered under this study.

Data were collected from the migrant households of sample villages with the help of personal interview method through pretested schedules and questionnaire. The questionnaire was specifically designed to collect data on variables like level of income, employment, consumption pattern, health status, level of education, awareness, exploitation, indebtedness, work - environment, working hours, wage discriminations, remittances etc.

The returned migrant respondents in their native village were identified through village survey at different intervals during May 2003 to June 2004.

Mostly, the head of the returned migrant household was interviewed to fill up the questionnaire. It was found that usually the migrant households migrate to different place with in the state and outside the state to work in the brick-kiln industries mostly in case of Bolangir districts, in case of Kalahandi to Raipur, Bastar and other places of Madhya Pradesh and to Andhra Pradesh in case of Malkanagiri district, during November. It was possible with much difficulty to contact some of them at their places of destination in the far of places in Visakhapatnam, Hydrabad, Bombay, Srikakulam, Ichapuram, Raipur, Bargarh (Sambalpur districts) and various places in Ganjam districts (Orissa) etc.

II

Causes of Migration

A large segment of migrant labourers in Orissa belong to the category of land less agricultural labourers and very often from scheduled, backward or tribal castes. In few cases those who have limited land didn't possess the needed resource to develop the same and as a result, the barren land is left uncultivated for years. Therefore, they are compelled to work as agricultural labourers in the land of the big landlords or Zamidars of the same village or adjourning villages. The employment being seasonal and the wages being low, they find it hard to make both ends meet. Thus, the insufficiency of such labourers' income to cover the living expanses even on a subsistence level seems to be the basic underlying factor of their indebtedness leading to mass migration in search of employment.

In the context of Orissa, the tribes constitute about 23% of the total population, live in abject poverty segregated form the mainstream of life. They are educationally , socially and economically for backward then other social groups.

Especially in the tribal dominated undivided districts of Kalahandi, Bolangir & Koraput (KBK) there are repeated cases sale of child, bonded labour, starvation death, frequent outbreak of diseases, mass drop outs, severe unemployment leading to mass migration etc. (Tripathy, S.N. 1989).

In the past forests was providing a source of living for the vast majority of tribes. Because of the Orissa forest Act 1972, the state has exploited the forest for commercialization and has drastically cut the rights of the local people and the tribes to use the forests and its produce. Thus, the businessmen, traders and contractors are at an advantageous position that could obtain the licence to deal with forest produce. Over the years, the tribes have lost their customary rights over the forests and the life support system and ultimately, forced to migrate to eke out a living in the distant land.

Another important factor is that most of the industrial units, mining operations, and river dam projects are located in the triabl concentrated undivided districts of Koraput and Bolangir. Either surrounded by deep forests, or agricultural land, these projects, provide a support for their living. But land acquisition by the projects have displaced these tribes from their original habitat, deteriorated their economic condition and led to landlessness, joblessness and homelessness.

III

Findings of the study

While in remittances from the out migrants form an important basis for transforming village life including introduction of new technologies and high valued crops. At the same time, the absence of a large chunk of the able-bodied population from the village, create the demand for immigrants form other, less developed villages.

It has been found that no-remittance household constitute 44.67 per cent in our study. Sample migrant households remitting within Rs. 2,000 and Rs. 2,000 to Rs. 3,000 annually are 19.33 percent and 13.67 percent respectively. Thus, remittances by the migrant households in our sample districts are not heartening. However, remittance to the household by the out-migrants considerably influence their living standard and could prevent the starvation death and provide the basic minimum needs to support their living or survival.

It has been studied that more than 62 percent of migrant household annual income is below Rs. 12,000. Annual expenditure of more than 39 percent of migrant households are in the range of Rs. 10,000 to Rs. 14,000. Thus, though 62% of migrant households earn below Rs. 12,000/- but about 40% households. Thus, there is indebtedness amount the tribal households. Thus, it is because of the migrants or urban migration the burden of debt could be minimized.

Migration could enable to recycle the process of obtaining loans from the contractors or money lenders. The migration could enable the migrant sample households in our study to repay the loans with interest and also to maintain their expenses during rainy season or day or unemployment in their native villages.

The occupational pattern of the migrant sample households highlights that more than 31 per cent households are cultivators, 47 per cent households are agricultural labourers, 14 percent households are engaged in 'other works' said business. Thus, most of the tribes in the sample districts depend upon agriculture; wage labour forest and other activities. Scantly rainfall, inadequate, unfertile scattered land holding are also responsible for inadequate employment and earnings of the migrant households.

It is revealed that about 60 percent sample migrant households are 'landless'. The problem of land alienation among the tribal households results in 'landlessness' and 'asset less ness' of tribal migrant households.

The study has further pointed out that about 90 percent of sample migrant households are unemployed for more than 4 months at their native villages. Data reveals that 66.33 percent of households remain unemployed for more than 5 months at their native villages.

Thus, it is because of rural-urban migration the tribes of Kalahandi Bolangir and Malkanagiri could be employed in the distant places in Andhra Pradesh and Madhya Pradesh or in the advanced regions of Orissa for their employment and income. Thus, rural-urban migration in our analysis provided assured source of employment to the tribes.

The migrant households experience better living standard. Therefore, we can infer that migration results in ameliorating the standard of living of the migrant households. The flow of labour from rural tribal region to the urban centre, as a result of out-migration has provided adequate employment and income to the households, which was lacking in the native villages of the migrants. By their exposure to the outside world, the outlook of the tribal migrants has been widened. They could experience the hard relatives of life and face challenges, problems during the process of their migration.

The rural-urban migration in the tribal dominated villages of Kalahandi, Bolangir and Malkanagiri has further revealed the media of migration. The response of the sample migrant households shows that the highest percentage of households (54%) have migrated to the destination place though the contractors and unlicensed agents.

In the sample village of Bolangir the media of migration is more influenced by contractors and unlicensed agents, among the sample migrant households.

Thus, we find that the system of advance payment[3] during/ the recruitment of labour for employment is a continuous process found in the underdeveloped process found in the underdeveloped tribal regions of Kalahandi, Bolangir and Malkanagiri in Orissa.

It has been observed that PDS has not delivered essential commodities to meet the minimum food needs of the drought-hit villages of Kalahandi, Bolangir and Malkanagir districts. A considerable amount of food grains and essential goods are supplied to the urban centre and sold directly to the businessmen by the dealers in a close nexus with the corrupt officials of the supply department. Thus, corruption has obstructed the noble objectives to deliver the essential food and other items to the rural poor.

An inevitable sequel to the insensitivity and absurdity of the food security system is distress migration from the drought-hit villages of Kalahandi, Bolangir and Malkanagiri districts to the urban areas.

As has been observed from the study the most important reasons for failure of economic development and removal of poverty in the tribal dominated villages of Kalahandi and Bolangir is corruption which is rampant causing 'leakages' in the amounts ear marked for rural employment generating schemes. When this happens the investments do not create the employment opportunities as contemplated at their initiation, nor do they result in goods and services being provided in proportion to the investments made.

As a result of which there is a vicious circle of poverty, unemployment, indebtedness and migration in the districts of Kalahandi, Bolangir and Malkanagiri districts. Lack of employment and distressed condition of living compels the tribal migrants to take advance from the contractors resulting in migration. The vicious circle continue unabated for decades in the these sample districts as the planned measures could not percolate benefits considerable in the rural regions of the districts.

Suggestions

In order to halt the process of migration, infrastructure development through irrigation, watershed management, road construction, forestation coupled with agro processing, rural industries, food processing industries, rural manufacturing, provisions of social securities, proper implementation of employment for the tribal dominated, drought-ravaged and poverty-stricken KBK districts of Orissa.

The urgent need of the hour is heavy investment in the traditional sector as well as in industrially backward region for adequate employment creation. Since modern manufacturing industries are expected to absorb only a limited number of labourers, adequate employment can be created in small-scale industries, construction works, labour-intensive road works afforestation, animal husbandry, fishery and the like.

NOTES

KBK districts basically refer to the undivided districts such as Kalahandi, Bolangir and Koraput and newly organized eight districts of Orissa namely, (i) Kalahandi, (ii) Nuapara (iii) Bolangir (iv) Sonepur (v) Koraput (vi) Newarangpur (vii) Malkanagiri and (viii) Rayagada, which are among the most backward districts of India. Total Area in sq.km: 47646

Total population: 63,20,4.68 (19.96% total state population)
S.T. population: 24,48,301 (38.73% to total KBK population)
S.C. population: 10,00,840 (15.83% to total KBK population)

REFERENCES

Tripathy, S.N. (1989): Bonded Labour in India, Discovery Publishing House, New Delhi.

Tripathy, S.N. and C.R. Das (1997): *Migrant Labour in India,* Discovery publishing House, New Delhi.

Tripathy, S.N. (1997): *Migrant Child Labour in India,* Mohit Publication, New Delhi.

Tripathy, S.N. and Soudamini Das (1991): *Informal Women Labour in India,* Discovery Publishing House, New Delhi.

Tripathy, S.N. (Ed.) 1999: *Tribals in Transition,* Discovery Publishing House, New Delhi.

Thorner Alice and Damiel (1962): *Land and Labour in India,* Asia Publishing House, Bombay.

Weiner, Myron (1978); *Sons of the Soil: Migration and Ethnic Conflict in India,* Oxford University Press, Delhi.

14

Education for Tribal Women

India has the second largest concentration of tribal population, after that of the African continent. The total tribal population of India as per the 1991 census was 6.78 crores which constitute about 8.08% of the total population of the country. About 90% of tribal population are concentrated in the central belt covering states like Madhya Pradesh, Chhattisgarh, Jharkhand, Bihar, Maharashtra, Orissa, Gujarat, Rajasthan, Andhra Pradesh and West Bengal.

Because of their backwardness, isolation, ignorance, traditional attitudes and illiteracy, the tribals are in the web of misery and stagnation. They have been victimised and exploited by moneylenders, traders, contractors and middlemen due to their illiteracy. In order to lift the poverty-stricken, exploited tribals from the morass of poverty and backwardness, there is imperative need of educating the tribals and more specifically women, which will empower them.

Moreover, the constitution of India provides as directive Principles of State Policy that the state should promote with special case the educational and economic interests of the weakers sections of the people and in particular of the tribals and should protect them from social injustice and all forms of exploitation.[2]

It is of late realised that the role of education as an investment in human resources has been increasingly recognised all over the developing countries. In 1973, the standing committee of the Central Advisory Board of Education agreed that every effort should be made at the elementary level, to enroll all children of scheduled castes and scheduled tribes. All necessary steps for the purpose should be adopted. These would include the tribal language, provision of special allowances and other facilities of teachers working in tribal areas, free supply of educational materials, clothing of mid-day meals, provision of scholarships and hostels when necessary, increasing number of Ashram schools, etc. The funds required for these programmes should be provided in the general sector on a priority basis.[3]

In the undivided districts of Orissa, tribals constitute about 57.87% in Mayurbhanj, 54.31% in Koraput, 50.74% in Sundargarh, 44.52% in Keonjhar, 37.32% in Phulbani, 30.96% in Kalahandi and 27.45% in Sambalpur. According to 1991 census, Orissa has 316.6 lakhs people of which 70.32 lakhs are tribal people. Out of the total tribal population 36.19 lakh are women (Pasayat, 1993).[4]

The literate population among tribal people works out to 12,72,363 (18.10% of tribal population), of which 9.81 lakhs (27.92%) are male literate and only 2.92 lakhs (3.32%) are female literate. It means more than 44.33 lakhs of tribal population are still illiterate. Of them nearly 18.63 lakh are males and little more than 25.65 lakhs are females. In other words, literacy of tribal women in Orissa is disheartening and deplorable. (Pasayat, 1999).[5]

It is essential to point out the literacy level during census period to understand the gap which exists between general children and tribal children with regard to literacy rate.

Table 14.1

Literacy Rates among Tribal and General Students in India

Year	Tribal literacy rates (in percentage)	General literacy rates (in percentage)
1961	8.53	28.30
1971	12.36	29.48
1981	16.35	36.23
1991	29.60	52.21

As per 1991 census, 29.6% of the scheduled tribe population in age group of 7 years and above has been found to be literate. The literacy rate being 40.65% for males and 19.19% for females in India. In the states of Andhra Pradesh, Bihar, Madhya Pradesh, Orissa, Rajasthan and Tamilnadu, the literacy percentage of tribals are 17.61%, 26.76%, 21.54%, 22.31%, 19.44% and 27.89% respectively.

Table 14.2
Literacy Rates among Tribal Dominated States of India

Sl. No.	Name of the States	Male	Female	Differential
1.	Bihar	39	13	26
2.	Gujarat	43	19	24
3.	West Bengal	35	11	24
4.	Maharashtra	39	15	24
5.	Orissa	32	9	23
6.	Madhya Pradesh	26	9	17
7.	Andhra Pradesh	22	7	15

General Differential

A glance at the Table 14.2 reveals that there is a great gender differential in the realm of literacy rates between male and females among tribals.

Table 14.3
Literacy Percentage during 1971, 1981, and 1991

States	1971		1981		1991	
	Male	Female	Male	Female	Male	Female
Bihar	18.45	04.83	26.17	07.75	38.40	14.75
Madhya Pradesh	13.05	02.18	17.74	03.60	32.16	10.75
Orissa	16.39	02.38	23.27	04.76	34.44	10.21

It is found from the Table 14.3 that there is a wide male-female differential in Bihar, Madhya Pradesh and Orissa—the major tribal dominated states of India. The increase in literacy rate in these three states are also not encouraging. Thus, the level of literacy amongst females is extremely low and more specifically among the tribals of our country.

Table 14.4
ST and SC Female Literacy Rates in India

Year	1971	1981	1991
Scheduled Castes	6.44	10.93	23.76
Scheduled Tribes	4.85	8.04	18.19

The All-India level data shows that while in 1971, the percentage of tribal literacy was 4.85% increased to 8.04% in 1981 and further picked up to 19.19% in 1991. Across the backward castes i.e. in between S.C. and S.T., the scheduled castes have better literacy rates compared to S.T.s.

Enrolment Ratio: Inter-group Disparities

At the primary level, the group enrokentt-ratios for scheduled tribe boys (6.11 age group) was 129.9% compared to 94.8% for girls. The variation among girls was higher (CV 37.23%) than the boys (29.55%). At the upper primary level (11.14 age group), 6.16 per cent boys and 37.6% girls were enrolled. Here also, the variations among girls has been higher (51.44% higher) than boys (34.72 per cent). (Pandey, 1996)[6]

The number of tribal girls enrolled in the primary and upper primary levels of Rajasthan, Uttar Pradesh, Madhya Pradesh, Bihar, Orissa, and West Bengal is negligible.

Enrolment Ratio: Inter-state Disparities

Gross enrolment ratios (GER) at the primary level, for girls ranges from 49.2% in Rajasthan to 171.1 per cent in Assam with regard to boys the percentage of enrolment in Bihar ranges from 90.7% to 19.6% in Assam. At the upper primary level (11-14 age group) the GER for girls range between 35.5% in Bihar and 116.3% in Assam. Three states of India, Bihar, Madhya Pradesh and Orissa accounting more that 44% at the primary level enrollment. The enrolment of girls in these three states is 62.8%, 59 percentage and 58.1% per cent respectively. The state of Rajasthan has recorded the lowest percentage of enrolment ratio (49%).

Table 14.5 reveals the total number of students and the number scheduled castes and scheduled tribes students alongwith the respective percentage at the primary, middle and high school levels.

Table 14.5
Total Number of Students and the S.T./S.C. Students Enrolled at Primary, Middle and High School Level

Stage	Total No. of students	No. of S.C. students	No. of S.T. students
1st-5th	86465189	13921012 (16.1%)	6580004 (7.61%)
6th-8th	28124756	3618480 (12.87%)	1282644 (4.58%)
9th-10th	116172662	1396712 (12.02%)	438742 (3.78%)

The table clearly shows that there has been high drop outs among tribal students after the primary education level (1st-5th) and the decline in percentage is 7.61% to 3.78%. The states which indicate a decline of more than 50% at this stage are Andhra Pradesh, Bihar, Madhya Pradesh, Orissa, and Tripura.

The Status of Tribal Women

The Verrier Elwin Committee (committee in special multipurpose tribal blocks) gives a picture of tribal women as follows:

"In most tribal societies women holds a high and honourable place. She goes proudly free about the country side. In field and forest she works in happy companionship with her husband. She is not subjected to early child bearing. She is generally married when she is mature, and if her manage is failure (which is seldom) she has the right to divorce."

Thus, the position of women in the tribal society is better than non-tribal society.

Observations

But is has been observed by the researches that in recent years, because of land alienation, poverty and lack of support system tribals in general and women in particular are in the web of misery, starvation and thus, leading a sub-human living. Moreover, there is apathy of administrative personnel, lack of political will in implementing tribal programmes. It is further observed that there are large number of one teacher schools, in the interior tribal pockets. The teacher never attends the school and the supervisor never supervises the schools. The teachers bribe the officials and receive their salary in tribal belts of Koaput, Maldangiri, Nowrangpu, Kalahandi districts of Orissa. The reality has not been reported in most cases. Due to lack of communication and awareness tribal children help their parents in income-generating activities. They work in the collection of minor forest produce, agricultural operations, beedi rolling, in brick-klin industries (Tripathy, 1997). The availability of schools in predominantly S.T. habitations is less those in, all habitations.

Now withstanding the revised National Policy on Education, and subsequent Programme of Action, implementation of certain aspects has lagged behind. Education for tribal people and especially the females among them, has not received the impetus it was expected to recieve.[8]

The age-old poverty of tribal is an important stumbling block in the way of tribal education. The tribal parents of repeat, always seek the assistance of their children in various activities rather than sending them to schools. Even when the children fail to clear the school examination, tribal parents never take pains to send their children again to school.9 Education persons, leaders the NGO's should play effective role in mobilising the tribal parents for enrolment. The leakages of funds in tribal areas meant for infrastructural development should be controlled. The researchers also observed that tribal children are engaged in teachers residences during off-time to work in various domestic activities, gardening, cleaning utensils etc. The executive visit of scholars in Chelligarh (Gajapati Dist.) Muniguda, Malkangiri, Kalahandi regions confirm this observation. Thus, the teachers appointed in tribal regions should have sincerity of purpose and dedicated attitude to serve the tribal children, so that tribal women literacy will increase. The education of girls will further accelerate tribal education in general as girls can motivate the members in the tribal community. Once the education of tribal girls are boosted up, it can act as a force to halt the growing corruption in tribal regions as all-developmental and interventional efforts of the Government can be fruitful.

Wastage and Stagnation

Various factors emerged as responsible for high incidence of wastage and stagnating in tribal regions. The vital factors being the lack of adequate consciousness among the older generation for the need of formal education. Next important factor is poor economic conditions of the bulk of tribals as a result of which all members struggle for sustaining their lives by performing labour.10 The economic value of engaging children in tribal regions joined significance due to object poverty rather than educating them. The problem of drink, disease and debt keep the tribals in perpetual indebtedness resulting them in the state of backwardness, illiteracy and ignorance. As has been observed, the important cause of high incidence of wastage and stagnating in tribal pockets of India are inadequate, insufficient, inefficient and insincere role played by teachers appointed in tribal areas due to ineffective and corrupt administrative machinery (observations in Orissa for the last 20 years). There are many personal and family reasons for more number of girl's drop out.

Hence, a change in attitude and dedication of workers, teachers are needed to increase the literacy rate among tribals and females in particular.

REFERENCES

1. Pandey, Jyotsana (1996), "Level of Education among Triabl Children", *My Name is Today*, Vol.IV, No. 3 & 4, July-December, p.14.
2. Indian Constitution, Article 46.
3. Manavi, M.I. (1999), "Human Resource Development in Tribal Areas of Gujarat", in Tripathy, S.N. (ed.) *Tribals in Transition*, Discovery Publishing House, p.105.
4. Pasayat, Chitrasen (1993), "Literacy in Orissa", *Orissa Review*, pp. 42-43.
5. Pasayat, Chitrasen (1999), "Need of Educating Tribal Children in Orissa", In Tripathy, S.N. (ed.) *Tribals in Transition*, op. cit., p.70.
6. Pandey, Jyotsana (1996), *op. cit.*, p. 16.
7. Tripathy, S.N. (1997), *Migrant Child Labour in India*, Mohit Publications, New Delhi.
8. Education for Tribal Women, *Social Welfare*, August-September 1995, p.59.
9. Pasayat, Chitrasen (1999), *op. cit.*, p. 78.
10. Masavi, M.I. (1999), *op.cit.*, p.108.

15

Empowering Migrant Tribal Women in Orissa

Introduction

A large segment of migrant labourers in Orissa belongs to the category of landless agricultural and very often from scheduled, backward or tribal castes. The inadequacy of employment in tribal regions causes insufficiency of income to cover the living expenses even a subsistence level. Further, the social customs and obligations like births, marriages, death in the family and drinking habits etc. cause indebtedness of these landless tribals. The moneylenders use that the advantage of the deteriorating economic conditions of the poor tribals. They advance small loans from time to time in exchange of binding them to work as agricultural labourers till the final payment is made. But the dues accumulate very fast under exorbitantly high rates of interest. They find it impossible to extinguish their debts by the hard labour. At this critical time, the Sardars or Khatadas—the recruiting agents of the brick kiln owner or stone query lessees or construction project contractor approach such tribal labourers. They make false promises, allure the poverty stricken tribal labourers to the distant land. The tragic fact is that, no sooner they reach at the worksite, then all the hopes disappear and promises made to them undermine. They are made to work pretty long hours, not being provided with medical benefits, proper food and shelter. Such laboures are mainly recruited from the rural and tribal regions of Mayurbhanj, Koraput, Kalahandi, Balangir and Phulbani districts. Thus, the problem of tribal migration is of serious magnitude as the problem of human misery, exploitation, indebtedness etc. are associated with it.

Moreover, due to deforestation, pressure on land, lack of irrigating, recurring drought, poverty and unemployment, tribals of Kalahandi, Bolangir, Koraput, Phulbani, the most backward tribal districts of Orissa migrants outside districts and state for a period of 4 to 6 months alongwith their wives and children to engage themselves in construction projects, brick-kilns and there unskilled manual works. The migrant tribal women usually migrate to Andhra Pradesh, Madhya Pradesh or West Bengal.

In the light of the aforesaid analysis, it was decide to focus light on the problems of migrant tribal women of poverty stricken drought ravaged district of Kalahandi (Orissa). Besides, Kalahandi districts is hitting the headlines of national newspaper for the bonded labour, starvation death, sale of child and mass migration.

For the present study the primary data have been collected from three sample villages on random sampling method from golamunda Block, situated at a distance of 170 kms. from the Districts headquarters in Hnarmagarh subdivision of Kalahandi district. The sample villages Nuamunds, Karko and Sinamal are located at a distance of 35,36 and 4 km. respectively from the block headquarters. The tribal households constitute 62 percent, 40 percent and 50 percent respectively in these three villages. In the absence of assured source of income and employment in these tribal dominated households, tribal men and women are forced to migrate distant places in search of employment. Data on various socioeconomic variables of migrant households with the help of personal interview through Schedules and questionnaire.

The large-scale migration of seasonal migrants from these three villages are due to failure of local support system. Due to lack of employment and income, they borrow from the contractors or Sardads with the promise to render their services in various worksites. Mostly tribal women are employment in construction works, brick-klins and informal sector inurban areas.

Profile of the Study Area Golamunda Block

Golamunda block is located at a distance of 170 kms., from the block headquarters in the Dharmagarch subdivision. It has the geographical area of 426.20 sq. kms., with 20,731 households. The total population of the block is 92,492 of which 46,173 are males and 46,319 are females. Out of 15,564 scheduled caste population, 7,729 are males and 7,835 are females. The percentage of scheduled caste population is 16.83 of the total population. The tribal population constitute 26.31 percent. Out of 24,339 Scheduled Tribe population 12,009 are males and 12,330 are females. (Table 15.1).

The literary percentage of the block is 23.16 which is much lower compared to the district average of 31.8 percent. There are 116 up schools found in this block. The total area of the block is 5355 hector. The total cultivable area of the block is 23,088 hectors, which constitute 0.88 percent of the district. The detailed land utilisation pattern is analysed in the Table 15.2. There is no major or medium irrigation project found in this Block.

Table 15.1
Profile of the Golamunda Block

Particulars	
Geographical area	426.20 sq. km
Total number of households	20731
Villages	
i) Inhabited	124
ii) Uninhabited	4
Total Population	92492
Male population	46173
Female population	46319
% of male literacy	37.12
% of female literacy	9.25
Total ST population	24339
ST male	12009
ST female	12330
% of tribal population	26.31%

Source. District Statistical Hand book, Kalahandi, 1993, Directorate of Economics & Statistics, Orissa, Bhubaneswar.

Table 15.2
Land Utilisation Pattern in the Golmunda Block

(Area in Hect.)

Forest Area	5,355
Miscellaneous tree crops and groves not included in the area shown	85
Permanent pasture and other grazing Lands	2759
Culturable waste land including gochar & groves	2131
Land put to non-agricultural uses	3126
Barrer and unclutivable land	153
Net area shown	23,088

Source. Data compiled, District Statistical Handbook, 1993, Kalahandi, P. 17.

Thus, we observe that because of extremely low industrial activities, the population of the block are agriculturally dependent, without any assured source of irrigation which causes flunturations in agricultural output drought and forced migration of the rural people.

Nuamunda

The village Nuamunda is situated at a distance of 35 kms., from the block headquarter Golamunda. The village has 60 households with a total population of 239. The detail caste-wise population of the village is given in the Table 15.3.

The village is a backward tribal concentrated village with 61.93 percent of tribal population. There is only an upper school in the village. The medical or postal facilities are not available to the villagers.

Table 15.3
Caste-wise Population for the village Nuamunda

Caste	Male	Female	Total
Scheduled Tribes (ST)	76	72	14.8 (61.93)
Scheduled Caste (SC)	13	22	35 (14.64)
Other caste	26	30	56 (24.43)
Total	115	124	239 (100.00)

Note: Figures in the parentheses represent percentage of the total.

The total geographical area of the village is 119.38 hectors out of which irrigated area is only 8 hectors. The unirrigated area is 54 hectors. The culturable waste including gochar and groves constitute 45 hectors whereas the area not available of cultivation is 3 hectors.

Karli

Situated at a distance of 36 kms., away from the block head-quarter Golamunda in Dharmagarh subdivision the village Karli has a total geographical area of 817 hectors. The land utilisation pattern of the village is shown in the Table 15.4.

The village has 240 households with a population of 1012. The tribal population constitute about 40 percent of the total population.

The village has an U.P. School but the medical or postal service are available at Golamunda block only. Out of the total geographical area of 588.82 hectors. A perusal of the study reveals that the sample villages are having extremely low percentage of irrigation facilities. Irrigation is mostly available through water-shed management, tank and other minor irrigation. Thus, in the absence of assured source of irrigation and employment in the villages, the tribals are forced to migrate distant places in search of employment as unskilled labourers. Thus, due to decline in land-man ratio, forest area, drought and lack of support system to earn their livelihood, the villagers mostly poverty stricken tribals alongwith their wives and children migrate to various parts within and outside the state.

Table 15.4
Land Utilisation Pattern of the Village Karli

	Area in hectors
Total geographical area	817.0
Forest area	186.0
Irrigated area	133.0
Unirrigated area	563.0
Culturable waste including gochar and groves	69.0
Area not available for cultivation	52.0

Table 15.5
Number of Migrant and Non-Migrant Households

Villages	Number of non-tribal migrant households	Number of tribal migrant households with female migrants	Non-migrant Households	Total Housholds
Nuamunda	20 (33.33)	12 (20.00)	28 (46.67)	60 (100.00)
Karli	74 (30.84)	54 (32.50)	112 (46.66)	240 (100.00)
Sinamal	68 (27.87)	52 (21.31)	124 (50.82)	244 (100.00)
Total	162 (29.78)	118 (21.69)	264 (48.53)	544 (100.00)

Figure in parenthesis represent percentage of the total.

Table 15.5 presents the list of sample villages with number of non-tribal migrant households, non-migrant households and tribal women migrant households. It is found from the table that there are 3 sample villages with 544 households in which a total 118 tribal women migrant households, 162 non-tribal migrant households and 264 non-migrant households. Thus, more than 51 percent of the households in the sample villages are migrant households, out of which non-tribal migrant households constitute 29.78 percent and tribal women migrant households constitute 21.69 percent.

Number of Migrant Households

It is found from the Table 15.6 that 50.85 percent households are having three migrants among the tribal female migrant households. Households with two migrants constitute 43.22 percent whereas only a meagre percentage of (5.93%) households have reported "four and above" number of migrants. Village-wise data reveals that Sinamal has the highest percent of (46.15%0 two migrant households followed by Karli (42.60%). Similarly, village Nuamunda has the highest percent of three migrant households among the tribal female migrant households in our study.

Table 15.6
Distribution of Tribal Female Migrant Households According to Number of Migrants

Number	Nuamunda	Karli	Sinamal	Total
—	—	—	—	—
	4 (33.33)	23 (42.60)	24 (46.15)	51 (43.22)
	7 (58.33)	27 (50.00)	26 (50.00)	60 (50.85)
	1 (8.33)	4 (7.40)	2 (3.85)	07 (5.93)
	12 (100.00)	54 (100.00)	52 (100.00)	118 (100.00)

Age-Group of the Tribal Female Migrant Households.

Age group of tribal female migrants are important from demographic and economic point of view as it has its impact on child reproductivity, labour productivity and utilisation of human resources. It is worth while to note that about 74 percent of tribal female households are within the age group of 35 percent years, out of which between 26.35 age group represent the highest percent (35.60%). Followed by 36-45 age group (20.03%).

The village-wise data highlights that the village Sinamal has the highest percent of (38.46%) migrants in the age group of 26-35, followed by both Nuamunda and Karli (33.33%) less than 6 percent of the total tribal female migrant households are in the age group of 46+ (11.7).

Table 15.7
Distribution of Tribal Female Migrant Households According to the Age.

Number	Nuamunda	Karli	Sinamal	Total
0-14	4 (33.33)	10 (18.52)	8 (15.38)	22 (18.64)
15-25	3 (25.00)	7 (12.96)	12 (23.07)	22 (18.64)
26-35	4 (33.33)	18 (33.33)	20 (38.46)	42 (35.60)
36-45	1 (8.33)	17 (31.48)	8 (15.38)	26 (20.03)
46+	—	2 (3.70)	4 (7.70)	06 (5.08)
Total	12 (100.00)	54 (100.00)	52 (100.00)	118 (100.00)

Figures in the parenthesis represent percent of the total.

Table 15.8
Distribution of Tribal Female Migrant Households According to the Main Reasons for Migration

Reasons	Nuamunda	Korli	Sinamal	Total
Search of Livelihood	10 (83.33)	38 (70.37)	32 (61.54)	80 (67.80)
Compelled by advance taken	02 (16.67)	16 (29.63)	20 (38.46)	38 (32.20)
Total	12 (100.00)	54 (100.00)	52 (100.00)	118 (100.00)

Reasons for Migration

The Tribal Migrant households reveal that search for livelihood is the dominant motive force of migration (67.80%) followed by "advance taken" (32.20%) (Table 15.8).

Level of Education

It is demonstrated from the Table 15.9 that the highest number of tribal female migrant households are illiterate (70.33%). Only 24 households constituting 20.33 percent have primary level of education upto middle school level.

Table 15.9
Distribution of Tribal Female Migrant Households According to their Level of Education

Level of Education	Nuamunda	Karli	Sinamal	Total
Illiterate	9 (75.00)	36 (66.67)	38 (73.07)	83 (70.33)
Primary School	2 (16.66)	12 (22.22)	10 (19.23)	24 (20.33)
Middle School	1 (8.33)	4 (7.40)	3 (5.77)	8 (6.78)
High School	—	2 (3.70)	1 (1.92)	3 (2.55)
Total	12 (100.00)	54 (100.00)	52 (100.00)	118 (100.00)

Figures in the parenthesis represent percent to total.

Table 15.10
Distribution of Tribal Female Migrant Households according to the Annual Income

Income	Nuamunda	Korli	Sinamal	Total
Below 15,000	5 (41.67)	17 (31.48)	18 (34.61)	40 (33.90)
Above 15,000 & below 20,000	6 (50.00)	30 (55.55)	29 (55.57)	68 (55.08)
Above 20,000 & below 25,000	1 (8.33)	7 (12.97)	5 (9.62)	13 (11.02)
Total	12 (100.00)	54 (100.00)	52 (100.00)	118 (100.00)

Annual Income for the Female Migrant Households

Table 15.10 exhibits the income of the tribal female migrant households. It is revealed from the table more than 55 percent of the households have income in the range of Rs. 15,000-20,000 in a year. Out of 118 migrant households, 40 female migrant households (33.90%) have the income in the range of below Rs. 15,000 per annum. Only 13 households constituting 11.02 percent have income level in the range of above Rs. 20,000 and below Rs. 25,000.

Indebtedness

Indebtedness leads to bondage and a type of contractual labour agreement between the labour and contractor or agent. Bondage leads to exploitation and distressed payment of wages. The indebted position of the tribal female migrant households have been studied in Table 15.11. It is depicted from the table that households without any debt constitute 9.32 percent of the total tribal female migrant households. Debt ranging from above Rs. 2000 to below Rs. 3000 constitute 43 number households (36.44%) of the total. The highest percentage of 48.30 percent of households have reported debt amounting below Rs. 2000.

Migrant tribal women households reporting unhygienic work environment constitute 63.55 percent, followed by disease related health hazards (36.44%), as depicted from the Table 15.12.

Table 15.11
Distribution of Tribal Female Migrant Households According to the Extent of Indebtedness

Magnitude (Rs.)	Nuamunda	Karli	Sinamal	Total
No debt	1 (8.33)	6 (11.11)	4 (7.69)	11 (9.32)
Below 2000	7 (58.33)	22 (40.74)	28 (53.84)	57 (48.30)
Above 2000 & below 3000	4 (33.33)	23 (42.60)	16 (30.77)	43 (36.44)
3000 & above	—	3 (5.55)	4	7 (5.93)
Total	12 (100.00)	54 (100.00)	52 (100.00)	118 (100.00)

Table 15.12

Distribution of Tribal Female Migrant Households to the Health Problem in the Worksite

Health Problem	Nuamunda	Karli	Sinamal	Total
Unhygenic work	7 (58.33)	32 (89.25)	36 (69.92)	75 (63.55)
Environment Disease adversely affecting health	5 (41.66)	22 (40.75)	16 (30.08)	43 (36.44)
Total	12 (100.00)	54 (100.00)	52 (100.00)	118 (100.00)

Figures in the parenthesis represent percent to total.

Conclusion

In the context of Kalahandi, 40 percent of people are landless. Among the landed class 69 percent are small marginal farmers owning just 31 percent of net cultivated area. It is therefore, suggested that there must be development of agriculture and allied activities to provide them avenues of employment and thus, halt the process of out migration.

A system of credit and micro-finance through Self-Help Group (SHG) should also be introduced so that exploitation in money-lending and exchange of commodities will be eliminated. This will go long way in breaking the nexus between the labour contractors and workers and provide inner strength and finally empower the migrant tribal women for Kalahandi. Corruption and leakage of investable resources should be controlled to get the desired result.

It is observed that tribal women labourers face instability and insecurity of employment, low wages and nonobservance of labour laws by their employers.

A major handicap for migrant tribal women labour is that they are scattered throughout the length and breadth of the contrary and do not have a single representative platform from which they can highlight their problems, unlike industrial workers who have trade unions.

It is therefore, suggested that the Migrant tribal women should organise themselves. Besides, they should also be educated, trained and skilled for empowering them as well as for increasing their efficiency. This will also pave way for waging a war against prevailing injustice, eroded value system and moulding their lives for change.

Index

M

N

O

P

R

■■■